A Traveller in Southern France

Christine Kaferly

A Traveller in Southern France

Copyright © 2012

Christine Kaferly

ISBN: 0615568343
EAN: 9780615568348
Library of Congress Control Number: 2011945702
Antiquities Research, LLC

To

Emma and Sydney

with love.

Table of Contents

Foreword

Several years ago, a good friend introduced me to the books of H. V. Morton who was, according to the dust covers, the most widely read travel author of his day. The scope and depth of the information contained in Morton's books on the United Kingdom, Italy, South Africa, Spain, and the Middle East revealed an extraordinary journalist and scholar. In reading about the author, I learned that he had been present at, and had written about, many of the great events of the early twentieth century, such as the opening of King Tutankhamen's tomb in 1922 and the London Blitz during World War II. His fame, his reputation as a journalist, and his personal contacts permitted him access to sites of historical significance that were closed to the average tourist. What I found most intriguing about his books was the breadth of historical background that he included with the descriptions of the places he visited. This historical context greatly enhanced my desire to visit whatever particular spot Morton was describing and to capture for myself the same feel for the past.

In reading more about H.V.Morton, I learned that his technique of travel writing stemmed from a habit he acquired as a young boy in England; when coming upon an old road, village, or ruined castle, he would wonder what the scene had looked like centuries before. This sort of youthful musing matured into an erudite and four-dimensional view of the world — the 'x, y, z, and t' of space-time — and informed his travels. He wrote not just about the common British or American travellers' destinations such as Rome, Naples, and Jerusalem, but also about the not-so-well-visited locations, particularly those that had great significance to the history of England. His books contained many references to little-known events that were related to much more famous figures in history. For example, he wrote about a village in northern Italy founded by the remnants of a Scottish regiment of soldiers fighting for King Francis I of France when French armies invaded Italy in 1525. Some of the events he included in his books were so obscure that I would search another source to check his facts; he was always right.

I made an effort to read as many of Morton's books as I could find. My friend and I compared notes on which volumes we each had been able to find in our local used bookstores. My first visit to Italy was greatly enhanced with the knowledge I obtained from *A Traveller in Italy* and *A Traveller in Southern Italy*. Both books were crammed with vivid descriptions, fascinating historical detail, and lively character studies.

H. V. Morton disappointed me only in that, as copious a writer as he was, he never wrote about France, Germany, Switzerland, or Austria; in other words, though he lived to a ripe old age, his writing career ended much too soon. I've often wondered how he might have written about those countries, and what his wit, keen observations, and historical research might have produced. Without having Morton as a guide, I have tried to conduct my travels in France and Germany using the Morton techniques of observation, and when coming to an interesting site, I have found myself wondering what the scene may have looked like centuries ago.

I love travelling, and I love reading history. I make a point of researching the history of a place before I visit, which increases my understanding and enjoyment, as well as enhances the memories of my trip. Combining travel and history seems to be in the best of the H. V. Morton tradition, but an approach not generally found in most travel books today. However, just knowing some historical facts does not address the "why"—why certain cities became powerful, why some areas became industrialized and others stayed rural, why battles were fought, why these events are important. History is a series of cause-and-effect connections, and the outcomes of these events have an enormous effect on the development of the land and the evolution of the culture—and the lives of the people. Connecting with that history is crucial to a better understanding of the people and their culture.

This book is my attempt to describe the experiences I gained over several trips travelling and living in the beautiful countryside in southern France around the valley of the River Cèze. These experiences and incidents represent several separate voyages to France, and have been collected and described without too much adherence to an ordered time sequence. This is not a strict day-by-day travelogue, but rather is a series of impressions of the region that inspired me to research the historical background. Similarly, the historical sketches I have included relate to whatever site or city I visited, and are not presented in chronological order. My history sketches jump around in time, from the fifth century AD to the first century BC to the sixteenth century and back to the ninth century AD, which is different from standard history books that present facts in sequence, from the oldest events to the recent. My peculiar way of regarding history, from the present backward into the past, derives from a search for causes, always wondering how things got to be the way they are. As a result, my observations of the present are intermingled with sketches of the past.

I have included two maps: one map of the major cities of southern France, and one map of the Provence and Languedoc-Rousillon regions. I hope these maps help the reader who may be unfamiliar with the locations and the cities I describe in my travels. My greater goal is to try to produce a description of Provence and Languedoc in an historical context that is both personal and enlightening, with as much accuracy as possible. I hope this account of my travels in the south of France imparts a fresh understanding of the people, their great country, and their dynamic history.

CLK

November 2011

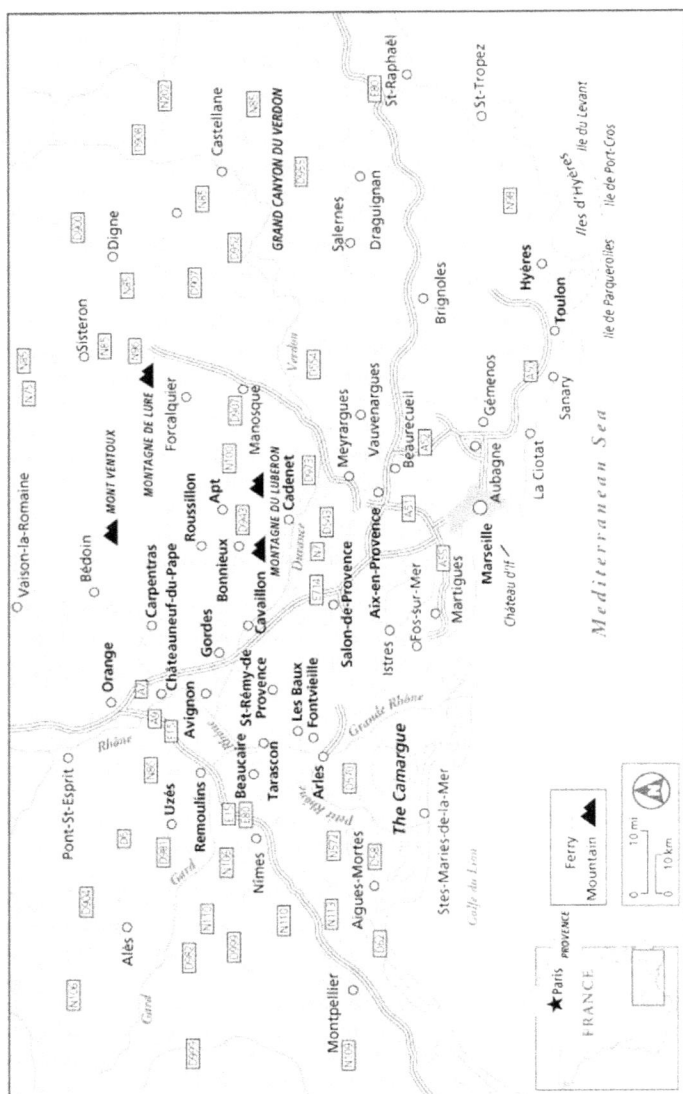

Map I: Cities in Southern France

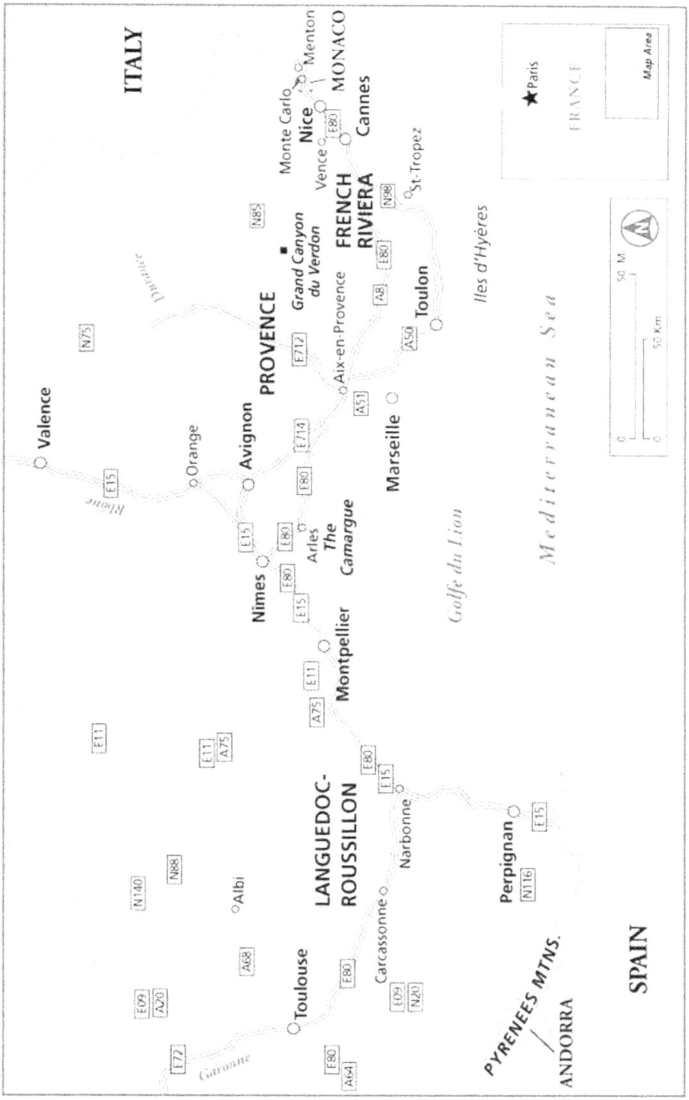

Map 2: Provence and Languedoc-Rousillon

CHAPTER 1

Arrival

**July in the Rhône Valley — The Village on the Cèze
— The House on the Esplanade — Sunshine and
Grapevines — Bicycling — Sunset with Wine**

The aircraft had started its descent into the airport at Nice, with the Mediterranean Sea sparkling before us and the western edge of the French Alps still dimly visible in the distance. Nice from the air was breathtakingly beautiful, and the landing approach gave us a perfect view of the famous *Côte d'Azur*, the French Riviera. The coastal land seemed crowded with modern high-rise hotels and luxurious vacation villas complete with swimming pools. As our flight descended, I could see the massive yachts moored in the harbors and marinas; some of the vessels were large enough to include a helicopter pad. Clearly this was the playground of the fabulously wealthy. The blue-green water came closer and closer until, at the last moment, I could see the landing strip. The runway seemed to be built on a landfill because the edges on the seawall were so manmade straight. I left the plane and passed through a glass walkway to the arrival gate in the terminal, and as

1

I walked I continued gazing out at the sea. Glancing about in the modern terminal, I could only imagine the royalty, celebrities, and movie stars who had passed through here with a look of bored indifference. Outside the terminal, the sea air, palm trees, and checkerboard-striped pedestrian crosswalks offered reminders that I was no longer in Colorado.

I made a stop at the ATM to pick up some cash in euros and had a *déjà vu* moment that was reinforced when I walked over to the luggage carousel to collect my bag. I had done all of this before, and my memory carried me back to the first time I came through this airport.

∽ ⌇

It was three years ago, and I was travelling with my daughter, Kate, to the south of France. Our destination was a small village on the border between Provence and Languedoc where we would stay at the house Kate and her husband, Marc, had bought the previous spring. The purpose of the trip was for me to become familiar with their house, get acquainted with the territory, learn the local customs, and acquire the necessary skills so I could make this trip on my own. So I had my first visit to the village the best way—with my daughter as my own private tour guide.

On that journey, we had arrived at the Nice airport at about five in the evening. We gathered our luggage, including the large bicycle case with my mountain bike, and caught the bus for the car rental lot. With what seemed to be a bit of Gallic humor, the rental office had two entrances, one marked *"Bienvenue Première Classe"* and the other *"Classe de Touristes,"* and both entrances led to the same reservation desk—*"egalité!"* The car we had reserved had already been rented, so we were hastily given a substitute— one without a full tank of diesel fuel and no windshield washer fluid, which I missed once we got on the *autoroute*, the four-lane divided highway, and were driving west into the setting sun.

The village

But what a beautiful drive! Provence in July is lush and green. We passed a succession of bountiful fields and farmlands that looked like they were tended with care and devotion.

We travelled for four hours over a variety of roadways that diminished in size: from the divided superhighway *autoroute*, onto small, two-lane national roads, down to one-lane blacktop, and then to gravel. Finally we drove up a very steep dirt road in the dark to reach our destination. The house, Kate and Marc's new home, is on the esplanade below the château in a small village in the Cèze Valley on the west side of the Rhône River. The caretaker, a woman of the village, had left the outside lights on, for which I was grateful, and had opened the thick, wooden shutters on the front door. In a state of exhaustion, we dragged our bags through the gate and around the upper terrace that rimmed the walled courtyard and then stumbled into the entrance hall. It was my first view inside the house that I had dreamed of and had seen in photographs, and I could hardly believe it was all real.

In spite of the cleaning the place had received in anticipation of our arrival, we found ourselves walking through cobwebs and wiping dust off the surfaces, not unexpectedly though, because this was midsummer, and the spiders, scorpions, and prevailing winds were untamed. We went through the house, opening windows and turning on lamps. I parked my luggage in the bedroom below the mezzanine that would be the library, and Kate set herself up in the master suite. We managed to eat a little supper before collapsing into bed, leaving the rest of the unpacking for the morning.

I woke up with the predawn glow coming through the open bedroom door; I rose and wandered through the house to discover what I had missed the night before in my fatigue. I made some tea, opened the door to the terrace outside the kitchen, and watched the sun rise near Mont Ventoux, just a silhouette on the horizon about forty kilometers due east. How exhilarating! Clear cool air, golden sunlight on the leaves of the grapevines climbing the stone walls, and the gentle humming of the wasps. The sky over the western hills was the startling blue that one might see in a retouched postcard. In the streets below the house, I could hear gravelly footsteps of early risers and could see the tree-lined Cèze River sparkling at the base of the village. The vehicular traffic over the one-lane bridge we had crossed in the dark the night before was controlled by a stoplight, the only one in town. I had been told the bridge was named *Pont Charles Martel*, and I was determined to find out why it was named for Charles Martel, the hero of the Battle of Poitiers and grandfather of Charlemagne. Across the river to the east, I could see an expanse of sunlit vineyards covering the valley, the neighboring towns across the highway, and the wooded hills beyond. How had this all come about? What fortunate sequence of events brought me to this lovely place?

Reflecting on the improbable set of circumstances that led me here, I considered how my daughter and son-in-law, while living in Berlin, loved to take cycling trips in the south of France and had resolved to find a house near their favorite bike tours. But how did they settle on this village? I remembered that they first explored this area when they stayed at a house owned by Marc's uncle near the town of La Gorce in Languedoc, and had discovered a lovely bed and breakfast called *L'Arbre d'Or*, the Golden Tree, in St. Michel d'Euzet in the Cèze Valley, also in this region. But the primary connection was the fact that eight years before my American daughter had met and married a young German who also loved travelling and cycling, and both of them thought nothing of driving fourteen hours from Berlin to southern France with their BMW stuffed with bicycles and gear for cycling vacations. I concluded, if Kate and Marc had never met, I wouldn't be here.

So I found myself in this amazing house, at the top of a village with remnants of thick stone walls built into the side of the hill on a limestone outcropping; perhaps it was originally a medieval fortress. Our house had the most amazing views of the village and the river below and, above the house, only the château. The village seemed to be perched on the hillside, with the houses built into the rock and constructed of the native, pale golden limestone and terra-cotta tile roofs. Because of the foundation on the steep, rocky outcropping, the winding streets of the lower part of the village, paved with stone and gravel, were only wide enough for one car. Higher up the hill, the streets became narrow switchbacks for pedestrians only. Sections of the ancient fortress walls and the round towers still stand and have become parts of houses or retaining walls that attach the buildings to the hill. Our house was built in tiers with each room occupying a separate floor. Behind the massive retaining wall in the courtyard garden was the dirt road where we parked the car. Above that loomed the château.

Across the crumbling footpath, at a mere arm's length from the courtyard wall, was the dangerous-looking stone wall of a ruined building, just a shell with the insides scooped out like an empty melon rind. I supposed that was what our house—perhaps the whole village—had looked like before restoration. The painstaking work of rebuilding in the village that started in mid-1950 resulted in a pleasing alloy of old and new, stone and tile and TV antennas. Most of the houses had terraces with huge terra-cotta pots and colorful flowers, patio furniture, and some clotheslines. The steeple of the village church was prominent and held the municipal clock that chimed the hour and half-hour. The chimes were repeated exactly two minutes after the first ringing, in case one miscounted the first time—beneficial to the workers in the nearby vineyards. After a short while, I became so accustomed to the bells that I seemed to live in half-hour increments.

The initial view of the village upon crossing the *Pont Charles Martel*, the Charles Martel Bridge, is so charming, with cypress trees nestled among the terraced stone houses and the château rising above it all, that the village is listed in the French publication *One Hundred and Fifty Most Picturesque French Villages*, from the association *Les Plus Beaux Villages de France* and, as a result, receives a large number of tourists in the summer. The tour guidebooks refer to villages such as ours as *vieux village des maisons de pierre*, meaning an old village of stone houses. "Stone" or "rock" in French is *pierre*, just as the name *Pierre* means Peter. I find it interesting how French retains the Biblical reference to St. Peter: "thou art Peter and upon this rock I will build my church."

Kate soon joined me on the terrace to watch the sun rise, and as the morning warm progressed to a midday heat, we realized we were famished for some fresh bread and vegetables. Kate also wanted a newspaper to get the latest news on the Tour de France bicycle race. So we got back in the dusty rental car and, again with me at the wheel, made our way back down the hill on the washboard-surface dirt road, which was scarcely easier to navigate in the daylight than in the dark. On the narrow, unpaved path with a steep drop at the edge, I had no idea what I would do if we encountered a car coming uphill. The dirt road ended at the edge of the village, behind the large stone municipal building, half of which housed the mayor's office, called the *mairie*, and the other half once held the school, but was later converted to a small library. In front of the *mairie* was the ancient communal washing tank, the *lavoir*, unused now with modern indoor plumbing and washing machines, but still nicely kept and decorated with pots of flowers.

During the day, the village was alive with tourists, workmen, and some local housewives, who smiled pleasantly. We passed the one restaurant, the *crêperie* Chez Babeth, which would not open until the lunch hour. The first time Marc and Kate brought me to this region was a July some years before, and we stayed in La Gorce, which was about eighty kilometers north. We drove down here to visit their friends in St. Michel and had lunch at the *crêperie*. It was my first view of this lovely village, and now because of Marc and Kate, I had a permanent connection here! I reflected on this delightful serendipity while we waited at the stoplight on the Charles Martel Bridge. We then drove back to the main road to the village of Goudargues, which had the closest grocery store.

Goudargues has a comfortable, old look of a Provençal-Languedocian village with the main street lined with huge plane trees along a canal, an ancient crumbling church, and shops and restaurants edging the town square. We found the market and loaded up on groceries; I let Kate do all the talking. Her command of French is impressive, considering she has spent so little time using it. Marc is even more of a linguistic marvel; he is a native German but speaks English perfectly with a British accent, and his French is very good. I can only aspire to be able someday to get by in French.

After we returned to the house, Kate dressed to go for her daily long bike ride, preparations for which always exhausted me. Because the street descending from the house to the bridge is so steep and rocky, I would walk down with her, carrying her cycling shoes while she walked her bicycle. She would be out for about two hours, and I was free to explore.

In what became a daily pattern, I spent my time wandering through the town and hiking the hills opposite the village with the large villas and swimming pools belonging to the weekenders from the cities. If I felt energetic enough, I would walk the four kilometers to St. Michel to pick up a baguette and a newspaper from the tiny shop there because there were no shops in our village. Sometimes I would ride my bike to St. Laurent, almost making the whole way up to the old monastery, the *Chartreuse de Valbonne*, without killing myself. The early afternoons were so quiet in all the villages, as if everyone were taking an afternoon nap. I visited the walled graveyards near the chapels in each village, which is my peculiar habit, reading the names and dates on the stones. There were graves of World War I veterans, and several had been honored with the *Croix de Guerre*. The graveyards in both St. Michel and St. Laurent were next to open fields, but our village graveyard had been squeezed in a small, level plot near the river. I thought it odd that the graveyard was so distant from the church, but I figured that because that land was relatively flat and had some topsoil, and the church was balanced on the rocky outcropping just as our house was, locating the graveyard next to the church was logistically impossible. The World War I monument in the village was a small obelisk placed at the crossroad just past the bridge and just before the climb into town. I made a point of reading the names carved into the pediment, and I repeated that habit with the monuments I found in the other villages. The Great War had left sad scars. Each French village, no matter how small, had its World War I memorial monument, just as I had observed in England and Germany. I wandered through forests and fields in the area, trying to imagine how it had changed over time and what it had been like ages ago.

In an effort to learn more about the village, I obtained a small history book, which I attempted to translate, that contained the story of the village. The history is mind-boggling to an American. The site has been occupied since the Romans built a fortified camp in the first century BC, and perhaps even earlier. One could imagine how the Gallic Celtic tribes encountered by Julius Caesar had exploited the hill's defensive position, complete with ample water, fertile fields, and woods full of game. The book claimed there was evidence of a temple with an altar dedicated to Mercury and Jupiter in the rough woods above the town. A marble plaque had been found near the château in the 1880s with the carved epitaph of one Aegrilia Florentina, which is now conserved in the Archaeological Museum in Nîmes. The centuries passed from the

Roman to medieval times, which brought a flurry of expansion and construction to the village. The critical centuries for establishing cities and great building projects seem to start at the twelfth, judging from the age of the castles and churches in this region. A certificate dated from 1156 by King Louis VII, called *le Jeune* and who was the first husband of Eleanor of Aquitaine, conferred feudal rights over the village on the bishops of Uzès, the large cathedral town about thirty kilometers to the southwest, whereupon the bishops started building. The village retains some very ancient buildings: the vault of the *seigneurial* chapel by the château dates from the eleventh century, and the château itself dates from the Second Crusade (1147–1149 AD). The village underwent successive waves of construction, fires, ruin, and reconstruction so common to the Middle Ages. The defensive position of the village was appreciated by the inhabitants during the Wars of Religion in the sixteenth century; however the Huguenots, led by the Constable of France, Anne de Montmorency, still managed to capture the fortress and burn the town in 1573. Montmorency was from one of the oldest and noblest families in French history. I wish I could claim to know him from reading history, but I confess my first exposure to the name was from the very humorous book *Three Men in a Boat (To Say Nothing of the Dog)*, wherein the irrepressible fox-terrier was named Montmorency. I have no idea why the author Jerome K. Jerome called the dog Montmorency; perhaps he did so because of some long-standing English antipathy with the French.

The book on village history implied that the French Revolution that started in 1789 had much less of an effect on the Cèze Valley than did the Religious Wars two hundred years before; those changes were mostly in the form of transferred property rights. Once the land confiscations that occurred during the Revolution were ended, the village formed cooperative bonds with the nearby towns, St. Michel, St. Laurent, and St. Gervais, with the villagers joining forces to continue the traditional agriculture of olives, cereals, and wine. The late nineteenth century witnessed the crisis of the phylloxera, the insect pestilence that destroyed the vineyards and exhausted the resources of the struggling farmers. According to the town history, the wine industry was fully re-established after World War I with the help of new grape plants from the Americas. The success of the grape industry displaced much of the olive cultivation, which had the unintended consequence of reducing the village population because the grape industry required far fewer workers than the olive industry. The population of the village never went above five hundred at its peak and is currently estimated to be about two hundred full-time residents.

During the crisis years, the houses in the village and the château all fell into disrepair. By the time Marc and Kate bought their house from the owner, it had already undergone extensive restoration and reconstruction. Most of the other houses had been rebuilt and the château had also been restored to its former glory. The previous owner of the house told Marc and Kate of a legend that it was originally the officer's quarters for the militia guarding the *seigneur*, the lord of the castle, and that a secret passage connected the house with the château. They showed me the purported entrance to the passage in one of the underground caves beneath the house. Curious as I was, I decided it probably would not be wise to explore the passage until I had at least made the acquaintance of the château's owners.

I tried to time the end of my hikes to coincide with Kate's return from her bike ride so I could meet her at the bridge with her sandals. We would walk back up the hill to the house together, exchanging a friendly *"bonjour"* with the people.

This was how we spent our days, with the occasional trips to the bicycle shop at Pont St. Esprit to service the mountain bike I had brought for myself. In the evenings, we would make some pasta and vegetables and open a bottle of the local wine I had bought at the grocers. The wines of the Rhône valley, *Côte du Rhône,* are famous, particularly the *rosé,* which lives up to its epithet of "sunshine in a bottle."

I could think of no more pleasant way to spend the evenings than settling into our patio chairs on the terrace with our wine and bread or pastries from the *boulangerie,* the bakery, in Goudargues, watching the sunset, and the moon rising full and silvery above the eastern hills. My favorite time of day at the house was in the evenings, lounging on one of the terraces after a sweltering, windy afternoon. The shadows would lengthen across the valley until just the tops of the hills clung to the last bits of sunlight. The patches of green in the vineyards would appear to have a richness of velvet, the forests would grow dusky, and the pale stone walls of the village would take on an amber glow, reflecting the color of the golden sunset clouds. The stoplight at the *Pont Charles Martel* became prominent in the twilight, and soon lights were flickering on in the village. At the stroke of ten, the *cigales,* the local cicadas, would fall silent right on cue. The birds' chattering stopped and was replaced by the silent bats as the air became still and languid. Occasionally I was able to observe the bats stir from their roost in the upper terrace and the treetops to begin their night of insect hunting. Their radar-controlled flights required a quick eye, and when I caught a glimpse of them flapping nearby, they amusingly reminded me of the Muppet bats on Sesame Street.

Many evenings I would move our patio chairs to the courtyard terrace below the walls of the château and watch the sky turn from deep violet to blue-black. Always thoroughly coated with insect repellant, Kate and I would try to read the newspaper by the patio lights, but instead we would find our attention diverted by the serenity of the night sky, the oleander bushes of pink and white blossoms, the cypress and olive trees, and the eleventh-century chapel next to the château with the floodlights illuminating the stone walls towering above us. When I switched off the outside lights, the stars would leap into view as would the distant lights from St. Laurent across the highway. We might have heard the far-away sound of a dog barking, perhaps the footsteps of a late-night tourist on the darkened path, but mostly the night was silent. Not wanting this to end, but our eyes so heavy with sleep, we would finally give up and go to bed. So tired…

∽ ⌒

Startled by the noise of a loud buzzer, I realized I was half-asleep, at the airport in Nice, still waiting for my luggage with dreamy memories. The conveyer belt began to move, and motley pieces of luggage appeared while the other passengers crowded around the carousel. I snapped out of my flashback and grabbed my luggage with a grim determination, knowing that I had a long drive ahead of me. I threaded through the Nice airport, made my way through customs, picked up the rental car, and got on the *autoroute* to start my solitary four-hour drive to the village. That first vacation here with Kate had been so relaxing, so effortless, and so comfortable. I wondered whether I could manage on my own. I was about to find out.

CHAPTER 2

Road Tripping

La Bourgnolle — Picnic on the Cèze — Stage 15 of the Tour de France — Loire Châteaux — Occitan

Alone, driving westbound on the A8 *autoroute* from Nice toward Marseille, I caught brief glimpses of the beaches and the sparkling Mediterranean, and drove by some of the loveliest resort cities in the South of France. Just the names were magical: Antibes, Cannes, St. Tropez. Leaving the seashore behind as I drove farther west, I had plenty of time to think and allowed myself to remember all the other European road trips I was lucky enough to enjoy with my daughter and son-in-law.

This was not my first, or even second, visit to *le Midi*, the South of France. After hearing Marc and Kate's tales of adventures and delights on many a bicycling vacation, I longed to be part of it, and they graciously invited me along on their next trip. By then, I had visited them in Berlin multiple times, in winter and summer, usually to coincide with vacations from their jobs. So I was privileged to accompany them on several of their marathon road trips. On one trip they took me along to the Loire Valley and Paris over a weekend, during which we visited many of the fabulous sixteenth-century châteaux. On another trip during Christmas week, we drove from Berlin to Mainz to see Marc's family, visited Salzburg, Vienna, and Prague, and made it back to Berlin, all in six days!

But the first time they brought me from Berlin to the south of France the destination was to be the house in La Gorce, a village in Languedoc-Rousillon. The house was owned by Marc's uncle, and we had rented it for two weeks in July of 2005. Because this would be a bicycling vacation, their BMW was stuffed with bikes, extra wheels, gear, and luggage. I managed to wedge myself into a comfy spot in the back where I could still get to the lunch bag to pass out snacks and drinks.

What a glorious road trip it was for me that summer. Starting from Berlin with our destination La Gorce, we crossed almost the east-west extent of Germany, watched the landscape change from the farmlands of Brandenburg to the low mountains of Thuringia, and passed through the industrial zone of Westphalia, across the Rhine to Mulhouse in France. We travelled through what had been the ancient kingdom of Burgundy, joined the motorway that followed the Saône River until it joined the Rhône at Lyon, the city where the Roman emperor Claudius was born, and continued south to the Montélimar exit. We then headed west to La Gorce, by this time in complete darkness, having done the whole 1,400 kilometer (almost 900 miles) distance in one day.

The house, called *La Bourgnolle*, had been a *mas*, an old stone farmhouse built in the Provençal style with small windows on the north side to minimize the effect of the fierce winter *mistral* winds. Marc's uncle had long-ago bought the *mas* in a state of disrepair, restored it over a period of years, added a swimming pool, and now used it for vacations and also offered it fully furnished to other family members on holiday. Marc arranged for us to rent *La Bourgnolle* for two weeks. Because it could sleep up to eight adults, the three of us had plenty of room. I had the upper level all to myself, complete with bath, sitting room, and a bedroom whose screen-less windows framed vine leaves gently creeping in from the outside stone walls. That vacation was the only time in my life I slept under mosquito netting, and upon waking, I was treated to the delightful sight of the morning sunlight shining on the leaves as the fresh breeze rustled them and rippled across the netting.

Breakfast, lunch if we were home, and dinner were all spent on the outdoor dining terrace, which was complete with a fireplace for grilling. Our meals were unhurried, shaded by an enormous umbrella by day and enjoyed under the canopy of stars at night. The *mas* was outside the limits of the village of La Gorce, so there was little stray light to prevent our viewing of the night sky. At times we were visited by the local cats or the occasional scorpion or lizard. Sitting on the terrace, we had an uninterrupted view of fields and farms, a few stone farmhouses, and in the distance the low, wooded hills. One could easily spend hours watching the change of sunlight and shadows on the landscape through the day. I recalled that the French Impressionist painters of the late nineteenth century praised the Provençal light and would strive to capture its effects on canvas. At last I understood why.

We made frequent trips for groceries to the nearest large city, Aubenas, where I was introduced to the amazing shopping experience of Carrefour, a WalMart with *élan*. We would buy meats for the barbecue, fresh vegetables and fruit, pasta, fine cheeses and wine, and my personal favorite, yogurt with chocolate chips called *straciatella*. We ate very well, primarily because we let Marc do all the cooking, and he's a great cook. One day we made plans to pack a meal and picnic on the Cèze River near the waterfalls called the *Cascade du Sautadet*, a picnic area popular with the locals. It was a great idea; the only problem was that we had no proper cooler, so the cheeses became very soft and odiferous in the car while we drove to the picnic spot. We resolved to find a cooler for our next outing, but finding a cooler that late in summer became a problem. We tried three stores, including the Carrefour that had thus far never disappointed us, but coolers had long since been sold out. When Marc vowed not to rest until he found the perfect cooler, Kate and I became concerned that the remainder of our holiday would be taken up with the search.

Because this was July during the Tour de France, and the *mas* had no television, the shopping trip when we, at last, found a cooler also gave us the opportunity to buy a TV that we could use to watch the daily race coverage on the France2 television network. Driving around, Kate had noticed a sign posted announcing a road closure the next day, the cause of which turned out to be Stage 15 of the Tour de France through the ancient city of Uzès, a city so close it was too good a chance to pass up. After consulting the maps and schedules printed in the newspaper's sports pages, we drove down to Uzès on the morning of Stage 15 and stationed ourselves on a particular roundabout just outside the town center to watch the *peloton*, including Lance Armstrong, fly past. We surmised that because this position was near a feed zone, the riders may not be flying past as fast as they would on the open road and we could get some good photos. Marc chose a spot at the top of a ninety-degree turn to get the whole *peloton* in one shot, and I parked myself on a curb to get as close as possible to the riders. As the crowd grew larger and rowdier, I had to elbow some locals who tried to get in front of me—I wasn't about to let any townies spoil a chance of a lifetime. My aggressiveness paid off. When the riders swooped by in a blur, I just kept clicking the shutter and only afterward checked to see what I had captured on my digital camera. And lo! There, neatly framed, was a shot of Lance Armstrong himself, no more than two feet away, surrounded by Team Discovery riders, and in the yellow jersey of the race leader. This would be Armstrong's

Lance Armstrong, 2005 Tour de France

seventh win and—supposedly—his last Tour appearance, so I felt very lucky to get that shot. We relaxed after the race with a picnic lunch in Uzès using the new-found perfect cooler.

The lasting impressions from that holiday were of vineyards and fragrant fields of lavender edged with stands of cypress trees; woods separating stone villages; wonderful food and wine; and sunshine and blue skies with the golden glow that has made Provence attractive to artists for years. Those two weeks were enough to convince me this land is heavenly—as in the German saying Marc told me during our picnic: *"leben wie Gott in Frankreich,"* meaning we were "living like God in France." As I watched Marc and Kate wade in the shallows near the watermill and polished off the rest of the cheese and Leffe beer while lounging on the riverbank, I realized what an improvement this means of travel was over my earlier experience of France.

∽ ✑

My first trip to France was an abbreviated visit to Paris, a nightmare due to my poor planning and need to travel on the cheap. I had failed to obtain adequate accommodations in a tourist friendly part of the city, and neither I nor Kate, who was in junior high school at the time, were comfortable in the fusty bed and breakfast that the guidebook had recommended—and the proprietor wouldn't accept my credit card, insisting on cash. I didn't know enough to request a room *ensuite*—that is, with a private bath—and as a result, we were given a cramped, charmless room and were forced to share a bath with strangers! Breakfast, which we had found to be substantial in England, was barely enough to sustain life until we could find a bit of lunch that didn't break the budget. Our knowledge of the language was so rudimentary that asking for or receiving information from the local *gendarmes*, the policemen, was nearly impossible. A typical exchange when we were lost and looking for the train station *Gare du Nord*:

"*Pardon, monsieur, où est la Gare du Nord?*"

Silence.

"*Pardon, monsieur, nous sommes perdus, où est la Gare du Nord?*"

Stony silence.

We considered continuing on by train to visit other cities in France but realized we would have to return to Paris to get back to London to catch our flight. And returning to Paris meant trying to find a hotel room having no reservations, marginal language skills, and no friendly faces to help. So, discouraged after only thirty-six hours, we took the train back to Boulogne, caught the ferryboat to Folkstone, England, and spent the rest of that holiday touring in the UK.

Kate and I had better luck travelling through Italy, and on another trip we spent a lovely ten days in Ireland. But Paris had left in me a shudder of memories.

∽ ∾

Several years later Kate graduated from university and met her future husband on a flight from Brussels to New York. The story is so romantic I love to recall it. She was returning from a semester of post-graduate school in Florence, Italy, and had taken a connecting flight to New York through Brussels. As she settled into her seat, a tall, young man with a crisp British accent politely informed her that she was sitting in his seat. She disagreed, whereupon he showed his boarding pass, which indeed had the same seat assignment as hers. The flight attendants quickly sorted out the difficulty and reseated them so they were sitting across the aisle from each other.

I'm told they talked for the entire eight-hour flight. When they arrived in New York, they went through customs in separate lines for US citizens and EU citizens (he is a German citizen). Marc told me later that the only reason he didn't panic at losing sight of Kate was because he had gotten her email address. "Smartest thing I ever did" was how he described his foresight. Some years later she found out that he had saved the stub of his boarding pass for that flight; she had saved hers also. A happy souvenir.

Their friendship and eventual marriage provided me with many opportunities to visit Berlin, where they were living. My first visit was only some ten years after the Berlin Wall came down. At that time my knowledge of German history in general and Berlin in particular was limited, and I resolved to do plenty of reading and research before visiting again. One basic question in my mind was why the capital of the Prussian state had been located in a marshy, sodden, alluvial plain with no natural defenses and grey skies for much of the year. I have since been able to piece together what I think are reasonable causes and effects for why and where Berlin exists, but that is another story.

Over the years my visits included some road trips with Marc and Kate so they could show me some of their favorite places around Berlin and Potsdam. One of the first multi-day road trips I took with them was to the Loire Valley in central France. I didn't hesitate for a second; they spoke French and would make all the bed-and-breakfast reservations. I didn't have to worry about a thing. Marc had toured the Loire Valley with his family when he was a youngster, and he wanted to show it to me. This was the visit that resulted in my improved comfort level with France. We conducted a three-day tour of the most famous of the Renaissance Châteaux: Chambord, the huge and magnificent hunting lodge of Francis I; Villandry with the beautiful sculptured gardens; Langeais, where Anne of Brittany and Charles VIII were married by proxy in 1491; Chinon, where

Joan of Arc met the Dauphin Charles in 1429; and Chenonceau, King Henry II's gift to his mistress, Diane de Poiters, which his wife, Catherine de Medici, confiscated from Diane de Poiters after Henry's death in 1559. We only had time for drive-bys at Blois, Catherine de Medici's château; Ambois, where Leonardo da Vinci spent his final years at the invitation of Francis I and where he died in 1519; and Ussé, the inspiration for the story of Sleeping Beauty and the original model for the Disneyland castle. Of course the excursions included picnics on the Indre and the Cher, and tours of Frankish medieval sites such as St. Radegund's cave in Chinon, where Queen Radegund retired to after leaving her husband, the Merovingian King Clothaire I, sometime around 550 AD. I still have the small vial of legendary miraculous water from St. Radegund's well, given to me by the shrine's elderly scholar guide and curator.

We left the *Val de Loire* region and drove home to Berlin via Paris. Paris! Anxieties from the past vanished as Marc and Kate gave me a driving tour of the city, after which we had a late lunch at a small café near the church St. Suplice and walked toward the *Ile de la Cité* to see Notre Dame Cathedral.

What an enormous amount of history in this region! After I returned home to Colorado, I started to read a great deal on the history of France to gain an appreciation of the connections that shaped modern Europe and to understand better the French contributions to the advancement of Western civilization. At that time I had no idea that my future might involve a closer connection to France with Marc and Kate's purchase of the house in the village on the river Cèze, near where we had picnicked by the waterfall that summer day.

∽ ∾

While driving through southern France, I realized again that the regions now called Provence and Languedoc-Rousillon had a different feel than what I had experienced in Paris or the Loire Valley. For one thing, the style of domestic architecture is Mediterranean, like what I had seen in Tuscany, with stone houses and terra-cotta tile roofs instead of the half-timbered framing with plaster and brick construction farther north. The climate is Mediterranean—sunny and dry—instead of cool, overcast, and rainy as it is in the north. As a result, the vegetation is quite different from the north, with cypress and plane trees lining the narrow roads that separate the fields of lavender, wheat, grapevines, and olive trees. The roadways were dotted with red poppies, and oleander bushes flowered near the small, stone farmhouses. Perhaps it was my imagination, but I sensed a certain attitude in the southern people, something that conveyed an air of separateness, as if the people of the South of France were more relaxed than the northerners and used to doing things their own way.

This should not be surprising, because what was the ancient region of Provence did not become part of the French kingdom until 1486, a thousand years after Clovis was anointed the first King of the Franks, and it retained its own language, called Occitan or Provençal, which is still spoken in remote areas today. Before becoming part of France, Provence had been in successive stages a Roman colony, part of the Visigothic kingdom, ceded to the Frankish kings in 536, then fell under the control of the Saracen Moors from North Africa, was annexed to the Holy Roman Empire, and was an independent duchy and kingdom up until 1486 when the Estates of Provence met to ratify the union of Provence with the French crown. By that time, the Occitan language (*langue d'oc, oc* meaning yes), which gave its name to the land, was distinct from the language of the north (*langue d'oil, oil* or *oui* meaning yes) and was fully established as the language of poetry and songs of the troubadours. I seem to remember reading how the Italian poet Dante briefly considered using Occitan for his masterpiece *The Divine Comedy*, instead of the Tuscan dialect of his native Florence.

That Provence had been Roman for centuries was still apparent; the major cities of Nîmes, Arles, Aix-en-Provence, Marseille, and Orange contain some of the best-preserved Roman buildings, monuments, and theatres in Europe outside of Italy. The Roman heritage of Provence is proudly displayed in the emblem of the city of Nîmes, an Egyptian crocodile chained to a palm tree. I think it is safe to say the Romans left the most enduring mark on the South of France, and the Roman way of life became intertwined in every aspect of Provence and Languedoc over the centuries. However, events and wars of the twentieth century did not leave Provence entirely unscathed; the German occupation in World War II is just one example. But even though the south became part of Vichy France, there is little to remind the visitor of the destruction caused by the German occupation or the Allied invasion in August 1944 to liberate the port of Marseille and southern France toward the end of World War II. No, the overriding impression of the south is Gallo-Roman, a timeless quality of unhurried charm and tradition.

෴

Why do I think understanding what went on here in the past is so helpful in appreciating what is here today? It may be due to my childhood education. As a kid growing up in Chicago, I understood, appreciated, and enjoyed my native city so much more after I had a fifth-grade class in the history of Chicago. I learned how the Iroquois and Illinois tribes lived in the forests around Lake Michigan and built their birch-bark canoes to navigate the rivers, how the European fur-trappers and traders first encroached on the land, and how Fort Dearborn was built to protect the settlers in what the people in New York and Philadelphia considered the Back of Beyond. Knowing the city's history opened my eyes and helped me understand why the city was there at all. Rather than learning a dull recitation of facts and dates, studying the history of Chicago made the city come alive for me, and I realized it was a story of people, the people who built a massive metropolitan region, made huge fortunes, changed the course of the Chicago river, developed industries and products, and expanded a frontier outpost to be the Second City.

History is the story of people. History helps us understand *why* along with *what* and *when*. Learning about the people who lived in earlier times helps us see that they were really no different—they had similar needs and aspirations: the desire for secure homes and property, a wish for better education and opportunities for their children, the need for good government and fair representation. Their civic obligations may have come under different terminology, evolving from feudalism to capitalism and nationalism, but they strove to achieve stability and prosperity as voting taxpayers do today. We can learn from the people who have gone before, from their struggles, their crises, their enterprises, and their failures and solutions.

The idea of regarding history as "lessons from the past" is not new. In this world of uncertainty, where we barely comprehend today and only can guess at tomorrow, the one thing we can attempt to know is the past. We have our memories, like Evelyn Waugh said in *Brideshead Revisited*, "for we possess nothing certainly except the past."

Why travel? Why study history? I believe humans have a fundamental need to know and understand more about our fellow humans and experience cultures different from our own. I am convinced there is no better way to satisfy that basic need than to travel and observe the way other people live. But there is more to it than that. Understanding people of other cultures requires some knowledge of their past. It is my belief that without some understanding of history of whatever country you, the traveller, are visiting, you may wonder why you've been dragged around from one castle or cathedral to another.

During one road trip with Marc and Kate, we stopped so Marc could grab a hamburger at a fast-food restaurant on the *autoroute*. Kate and I both wisely declined.

"So how was it?" asked Kate, knowing full well the answer.

"Blah," Marc responded. "Once you've had a hamburger in America, nothing else is as good."

"Hate to say I told you so," Kate responded.

Here's the point: enjoy international travel for the history, culture, art, and architecture because you probably won't like the hamburgers.

∽ ∾

While my mind wandered over the past road trips I'd taken, I realized that I had made the highway exchanges at Marseille from the A8 northbound onto the A7 without too much trouble, and I was now following along the Rhône River. Each *sortie*, highway exit, was posted with names rich in history and culture: Salon de Provence, Nîmes, Arles, St-Remy-de-Provence, Châteauneuf-du-Pape, Avignon, Orange. My excitement rose the closer I got to my exit, Bollène, where I left the *autoroute* and crossed the Rhône westward toward Pont St. Esprit. By now it was dusk, and I had to decide whether to take the scenic route past the *Chartreuse de Valbonne* or toward Bagnols sur Cèze. My cell phone rang; it was Kate wondering where I was and worried that she hadn't heard from me.

When I arrived in the village, by then in complete darkness, I did the best I could driving through the quiet village up the steep gravel road toward the château and parked next to the courtyard wall above the house. Again, the caretaker had left the outside lights on and had unlocked and opened the heavy shutters on the front door for me. I unloaded my luggage, not quite believing I had made it.

CHAPTER 3

An Ancient Land

**Prehistory of Provence — Musée D'Orgnac —
Looking for Dolmens**

What is it about Provence that makes it so distinctive? When we think of the South of France, we may think of the Cannes Film Festival or Monte Carlo and Monaco, as photographed in the Hitchcock movie *To Catch a Thief*. But modern attractions can mask a territory's intrinsic character that takes centuries to develop. Provence did not become Provence just because Europe needed another sunny playground, but rather it evolved over many generations. Just using my casual observations, I could see that this land of the Rhône Valley has supported human habitation for millennia. The Cèze is a tributary of the Rhône River, one of the great waterways of Europe, and served as the entryway into Provence and the interior of Gaul for the Romans. In fact, the name Provence comes from the Roman name given to this land, the first province Rome acquired outside of Italy. But how did the Romans know this was here? Was it because the Greeks had colonized the Rhône River delta six hundred years before? But how did the Greeks know about this lush land? And who met the Greeks when they were getting off their boats? How far back did I have to go to satisfy my curiosity?

I planned on using the three glorious weeks of summer alone at the house below the château to gain some understanding of this region. I had given myself a personal challenge to see whether I could survive alone, without my French-speaking children to guide me. The previous winter I had enrolled in yet another intermediate French class at the local university to brush up on my grade-school French, and I did as much reading as I could to prepare. I wanted to visit out-of-the-way places that the typical American tourist might never see. I wanted to explore in my own unhurried way the places I had seen from the back seat of the speeding BMW. My destinations were any and all the Neolithic, ancient Gallo-Roman, and medieval sites that I could get to in a one-day car trip from the village.

Before I could set out, some domestic duties needed attention. I spent the first days at the house cleaning. The house had been unoccupied since the previous October, and there were cobwebs, scorpions, and assorted bugs to gather up. The garden was overgrown with weeds and covered with last autumn's leaves. After I got the kitchen in order, I climbed back in the car, wound back down the mountain, and found my way to the supermarket in Bagnols sur Cèze for milk, eggs, butter, bread, meat, and vegetables for dinner.

After I had my living quarters under control, I was ready to start my one-day excursions, which would require some planning. The village historian, who ran the *Maison de Patrimonie et Histoire*, the museum of local history, provided me with brochures and other materials on the region, including her book, *A Visitor's Guide*, which was full of great historical information.

On one of my visits to the *Maison de Patrimonie et Histoire*, I found some brochures of the Val de Cèze that described the villages and

6000-year-old dolmen

some interesting places to tour. My imagination was captured by some photographs of dolmens and *bories,* the rustic dwellings and workshops dating back thousands of years and made by people from the Neolithic to medieval times. I decided that on my next excursion day I would try to find the dolmens that were in the heart of the Cèze Valley.

But first I had to learn the prehistory of Provence and gain an understanding of what life was like here tens of thousands of years ago. Fortunately, there was a fantastic resource for educating oneself about early man in this region, called the *Musée Régional de Préhistoire—Orgnac-Grand Site de France,* an education center and a museum of prehistory. The center was built next to the Aven d'Orgnac, the huge underground caverns in the Ardèche River Valley, of which geologists date the formation to 110 million years ago. The caverns are quite popular with spelunkers and school groups, and the tours, which were offered daily, took from three to eight hours, and were usually full. I was not interested in descending 120 meters underground among the chilly stalactites and stalagmites and with all those people. Instead I spent an afternoon in the museum, walking through the exhibits, reading the timelines of human development, and studying the artifacts and the dioramas. The full story of how this land was domesticated stretches far into the past, and the *Musée d'Orgnac* was a great help in getting a good grasp of prehistory so I could more fully appreciate how Provence came to be Provence.

I had always wondered exactly how and when *Homo sapiens* migrated into the various regions of Europe. The well-known "Out of Africa" theory of human migration describes how the species *Homo* first spread out from the area around modern Tanzania, moved north along East Africa toward Egypt, crossed the Red Sea into the Arabian Peninsula, across the Levant, into Mesopotamia and Anatolia, the Black Sea, and spread to India. These migrations took place over millions of years, starting about 3.5 million years ago. A timeline at the *Musée d'Orgnac* gave a date between 780 and 860 thousand years ago for the European appearance of the first *Homo erectus*, remains of which were discovered in northern Spain, and about 400 thousand years ago for *Homo erectus* in France, discovered at Terra Amata near Nice. The first traces of Neanderthals found in France date to about seventy thousand years ago. Neanderthals were named for the Neanderthal Valley near Dusseldorf, Germany, where the fossils were first found in 1856.

What impelled these prehistoric hominids to leave their homelands in Africa and wander off? Most likely it was the same sort of impetus as today—overpopulation and scarce resources, perhaps driven by changes in climate brought on by successive Ice Ages.

The progress of human migration into Europe was complicated by the presence of ice sheets, periodically encroaching and receding, one of many Ice Ages. From about 65,000 to 55,000 BC, there is little or nothing in the way of direct records of *Homo sapiens* activity in Europe, possibly because evidence of human activity had been wiped out due to the cold and ice. Using admittedly sketchy evidence, scientists believe that around 40,000 BC a warming period began, and these *Homo sapiens*, whose progress had been blocked by ice, first emerged from Central Asia, moving in a general westward direction, populating areas where the ice was receding. Wall maps in the *Musée d'Orgnac* showed these migrations with large vague arrows pointing out from Central Asia toward Central Europe. Those early humans who reached Europe gave rise to the culture called "Aurignacian" from the location in France where traces of it were first discovered. These early humans would have come in contact with the indigenous Ice Age Neanderthals, who inexplicably died out around 30,000 BC. The extent of these *Homo sapiens* interactions with the Neanderthal is still in dispute, but recent genetic DNA analysis suggests they were not completely segregated. Then the warm interglacial period ended, and from about 20,000 to 17,000 BC, glacial ice sheets in Europe grew to the extent that only pockets of habitable regions remained, including Italy, southern France, and northwest Spain, with Italy isolated from the rest of Europe by the Alpine ice. In this geological period called the Last Glacial Maximum (LGM), the sea level was about 120 meters (400 feet) lower than modern times, and the British Isles were joined with the European continent by a land bridge. The early humans in these regions developed their own cultures, the Solutrean around 20,000 BC and the Magdalenian around 18,000 BC, both named for regions in France where the artifacts of these cultures were first discovered. When the European glaciers started retreating after 17,000 BC, the humans of the Magdalenian culture gradually moved north, reaching and repopulating what is now Germany and the Netherlands and crossing into southern England. Linguistic and DNA evidence suggest that western Britain and Ireland were settled by Solutrean people from northern Spain, who built boats to skim the coastal waters of Western Europe.

I find it fascinating that France could justifiably claim to contain the entire, uninterrupted record of early man in Europe, just from the fact that the names of all these early cultures are derived from locations in France. For example, Cro-Magnon man was named for Cro-Magnon in the Dordogne River valley in southwest France where the first skeletons were found in 1868. The Cro-Magnon of the Paleolithic era on the evolutionary scale can be separated into distinct cultures. The Aurignacian Culture (32,000–26,000 BC) was named from Aurignac in the Haute Garonne area. This culture has been associated with the first modern humans in Europe, who produced cave paintings, stone tools, and small, sculpted figurines that were half animal and half human. Here in the Ardèche Valley, which is just north of the Cèze River Valley, the Chauvet Cave was discovered in 1994; the cave contains some of the earliest known cave paintings, dated to about 30,000 BC, and was the subject of the documentary film, *Cave of Forgotten Dreams*. The concurrent Gravettian Culture (28,000–22,000 BC) was named for the site of La Gravete, also in the Dordogne Valley. The Gravettian Culture artistic achievements included stone tools and "Venus" figurines. The Magdalenian, from La Madeleine, an Upper Paleolithic rock shelter in the Vézère Valley in the Dordogne, flourished from 18,000 to 10,000 BC, toward the end of the last Ice Age. To the Magdalenians we owe the cave paintings of Altamira in Spain and Lascaux in the Dordogne. The Solutrian Culture (19,000–16,000 BC) was named after a rock near Mâcon, France, and is characterized by flint blades, weapons with serrated edges, and the appearance of needles with eyes. A recent, highly controversial theory has put forth the suggestion that people of the Solutrean culture may have crossed the Atlantic, skimming the shores and glacial edges of ice west from Ireland, and introduced what is called the pre-Clovis culture (named for Clovis, New Mexico, not the Merovingian King Clovis) into North America, but this theory is not supported by genetic DNA analysis in studies of the peopling of the Americas.

The Neolithic period in Europe from about 7500 BC marks the shift from hunter-gatherer cultures to settled agricultural societies, the transition from living in caves to the building of communities, the domestication of animals, the production of pottery, and the discovery and use of metals. The *Musée d'Orgnac* had a very interesting exhibit detailing how Neolithic pottery was made from the local clay soil to which the potters had added crushed terra-cotta for strength. Those early people had figured out that storing grain in the pots kept foods safe from insects, mice, and humidity-spoilage. Even before the invention of a potter's wheel, these potters were able to form and decorate intricate pots and fire them in crude kilns to make an early ceramic, the first example of an artificial material in Europe. It is not known just how these early people discovered metal working. The early Neolithic potters knew how to transform clay into ceramics using fire; perhaps they tried other materials out of curiosity. We can imagine them thrusting rocks embedded with raw copper into their kilns and seeing the molten metal pool on the bottom. Metallurgy was born when people noticed improvements to copper with the addition of a small amount of tin, making a bronze alloy. Products from jewelry to weapons were now possible, and the technology spread. What we now call the Bronze Age was brought to France from Central European people, along with domesticated horses, around 2000 BC.

Precisely how agriculture arose in Europe and specifically southern France is still debated. One prevailing theory is the indigenous people discovered the techniques of agriculture; the other theory is outsiders from the Middle East or from the upper Danube in southeast Europe came with the new technology. In either case, archaeological evidence shows the gradual shift from hunting to agriculture, probably by 5000 BC. The Late Stone Age people, identified by the designs on their pottery, slowly evolved primitive farming communities and a language that has been called Proto-Indo-European. From these communities came the builders of the megalithic monuments in Western Europe. The stone alignments scattered throughout Western Europe, which demonstrate some knowledge of solar calendars necessary for predicting the timing of planting and harvesting, were the forerunners of the magnificent stone megaliths at Stonehenge in England, Carnac in Brittany, and at Newgrange in Ireland. These megaliths and dolmens are a distinctively European achievement, owing little or nothing to Middle Eastern inspiration, and indicate the early influence of the stabilizing effects of agriculture. The maps in the *Musée d'Orgnac* showed there were dolmens all over southern and southwest France, and I was now sufficiently prepared and motivated to find at least one.

The prehistoric cultures of Western Europe did not remain isolated; there is evidence of early commercial contact with other Mediterranean cultures. The European Bronze Age started around 1700 BC, and the metallurgy industry was supported by the Aegean's large-scale, widespread commercial trading system. This is known because artifacts of metal goods using ore not native to Europe but originating from the eastern Mediterranean have been discovered in southern Europe. The archaeological evidence gleaned in studying the grave goods from this period indicates increasing wealth and the emergence of recognizable chieftains with accompanying social orders—a very early aristocracy. Because of the Bronze Age industries, evidence of continued trading contacts between the civilizations of the eastern Mediterranean and Western Europe can be detected as early as 1400 BC. While Greece entered its Dark Age with the collapse of the Mycenaean civilization in 1200 BC, Western Europe was sufficiently stable and in a period of economic progress identified with the Urnfield cultures of the Late Bronze Age. (The name Urnfield comes from their practice of burying the ashes of their dead in urns.) By 800 BC there is evidence of settled farming throughout Western Europe based on plough, stock breeding, and specialized craftsmen such as metalworkers and pottery workers. On the dark side, the increased population density led to land disputes and hostile competition between separate communities. Hence we see the beginnings of the hilltop forts the Romans called *oppida*, defensive structures surrounding dwellings built with earthen or stone ramparts as protection from raiding neighbors.

Iron reached Western Europe around 700 BC, about six hundred years after the Hittites in Anatolia, modern Turkey, first produced it. Current theories suggest the spread of the use of iron was mainly by the process of cultural diffusion where, initially, traders from the East sold iron implements to the Europeans, and then small groups of immigrants settled and taught the iron production technology. It has been suggested that the use of iron in parts of southern Europe was first introduced by Phoenician or Greek colonists. We begin to see the causes and reasons for the presence of Greek settlements in the Rhône River delta; a combination of commercial motives and overpopulation in Greece led to the need for colonization. During the eighth and seventh centuries BC, the Greeks established colonies in Turkey, North Africa, Sicily and southern Italy, and southern France. The Greek colony of Massalia, the modern city of Marseille, was founded around 600 BC to open up and increase the movement of trade goods upstream on the Rhône and Saône rivers, and from there across to the Danube and the Rhine River Valley. As part of the extensive trading activity with the indigenous people of the Rhône Valley, the Greeks introduced olive and grape cultivation, the production of which continues to this day.

So who were the people who met the Greeks getting off their boats? They were Celts, who the Romans called Gauls. Evidence of the earliest European culture, called the Beaker People, appeared around 2000 BC followed by the Late Bronze Age Urnfield culture, around 1200 BC. The Late Bronze Age Urnfield culture was important for the history of Provence because anthropologists identify this culture as the source of the Celts. By 500 BC the population of Western Europe was speaking a variety of languages that have been identified as Celtic. Western Europe had developed Iron Age cultures called Hallstatt from its location in Austria where artifacts were first discovered in 1846; then Hallstatt evolved into the La Tène named from artifacts found near Lake Neuchâtal in 1858 in what is now Switzerland. By around 700 BC, the Hallstatt and Le Tène cultures of the Celts had spread over much of Western Europe, from southwest Spain across southern France, up to the British Isles and eastward to Germany.

And so passed the centuries, by the hundreds, during which the people of these cultures were born, lived, had families, worked, and died in their forest communities, living off domesticated animals and the products of their agriculture. There was no written language, but what later became literary traditions and ancient legends were transmitted orally. By the time the Greek traders tied their boats at the Rhône delta, these people, whom the Greeks called *keltoi*, were advanced enough to make attractive trade partners. They had cattle, woven cloth and animal skins for clothing, grains, lumber, and fine iron implements for weapons. Even though no written material has survived from this period, it is believed that the Greeks carried writing with them when they colonized Provence, and that skill of writing was transmitted to the Celts. According to the *Musée d'Orgnac*, Prehistory ended at the close of the Bronze Age, and the introduction of writing marks the transition from Prehistory to the historical era of Provence.

The Celtic La Tène culture, with the help of the Greeks, developed the defensive hilltop settlements called *oppida*, the remains of which can be found scattered around Western Europe, including a small *oppidum* near our village. The Gallic Celts built these settlements on the high ground near their agriculture lands. The communities also supported a variety of crafts, evidence of the specialization of labor that results from a surplus of food. Labor and trade encouraged building; villages sprang up. The European urban life had begun.

༄ ༄

One bright morning after a breakfast of tea and baguette on the kitchen terrace, I set out to find a dolmen. A brochure from the *Maison de Patrimonie et Histoire* describing the sites in the *Vallee de la*

Cèze provided a map and directions to a town called Méjannes-le-Clap in the center of a large forested area, which seemed to be a recreational forest preserve for hiking and horseback riding. I arrived at the information center and was able to get detailed instructions on how to find not only dolmens, but *bories*, the dry-stone huts used over the centuries by the *charbonnieres*, the charcoal makers.

I was glad to have a car because the forested area was quite extensive with few roads and fewer road signs. In the intense sunshine, the midday heat felt like a sauna, and the bushes hummed with the *cigales* and crickets. The dry heat reminded me of the southwest United States, perhaps southern Colorado, Utah, or New Mexico. I was quite alone in the forest, and when I came upon my first *borie* and parked the car in the adjacent parking lot, mine was the only vehicle there. I reached for my camera and got a few snaps. This *borie* showed the distinctive cone-shaped cap, about 1.5 meters in diameter and maybe 2 meters high, looking something like a beehive perched on a cylinder with a small, low door but no windows. At least this one had no windows. The flat stones were arranged in layers, built straight up to about shoulder height, and then the stones were arranged in ever-narrowing circular layers creating a dome. No mortar was used to secure the stones, a building technique called "dry stone," a style that is fairly common in southern Europe. I could find no plaques or markings, other than one proclaiming this to be a *borie* dated from about 1500 AD. *Oh, that recent,* I thought, laughing at myself for being so unimpressed with the age, since I lived in a city in Colorado in which the oldest buildings dated from the 1880s. I had read that these small buildings sheltered the *charbonnieres*, the charcoal makers, from the weather while they were roasting logs and tree branches in airless heaps to make charcoal. The charcoal makers were an essential element in the iron industry because the foundries that produced iron required intense heat, around 1000 degrees Celsius, a temperature that could not be reached without charcoal. Iron working as a craft had been an important industry since at least 700 BC, resulting in an ever-increasing need for charcoal. I wondered if the charcoal makers had been aware of the consequences of chopping down forests. I remember being taught in grade school that the deforestation of Western Europe, and especially England, was a result of the ship-building industry; huge tracts of forests were chopped down for lumber. If my teacher also mentioned that charcoal making, in creating fuel for the iron industry, was also a contributing cause to deforestation, I did not remember.

I wandered along a foot path and discovered a re-creation of a *charbonniere*. In a clearing I saw what looked like a large heap made up of small branches that had been bundled into a low dome-shape pile covered with sod and dried mud, measuring about four meters in diameter. A cutaway view showed how air was forced into the fires beneath the dome to create charcoal from the burning branches and small logs. The amount of air in the fire had to be controlled to provide just enough combustion to force out the water and resins in the raw wood to turn it into charcoal. The process had to be carefully tended and was very time-consuming, hence the need for temporary shelter. It was fascinating to think that here was evidence of an ancient technology, at least 2,500 years old, and which perhaps is still in use in rural areas today.

But now I had to find the dolmen. I drove to what the map indicated was the trail head of a hiking path, along which I should find at least two dolmens. I wasn't sure how much faith I should put in the distance indicated on the map. If it was really only 1.6 kilometers, maybe the hike wouldn't kill me; if it was much farther, the hike could be blister-inducing. With a fresh bottle of water, I set out through the forest, believing myself to be traversing land that had been home to a Neolithic people from thousands of years ago. It wasn't difficult to feel I had stepped back in time—there were no cars around, no machinery noises, not even any aircraft flying overhead. When at last I came upon the first dolmen, I was startled. The interior was far smaller than I had expected, barely large enough for two people to huddle together. It was constructed with four huge, flat boulders, three upturned on end to make the walls and one perched on the top edges to make a roof. The size of the stones that made up the walls and the roof was amazing; they must have weighed hundreds of pounds. The placard that had been set on the approach path read in French, "*Il y a 6000 ans...*," meaning the structure had been built six thousand years ago. A series of diagrams showed a cutaway view of how the dolmen had looked originally, that the large stones of the walls and roof had been covered with dirt and a layer of sod for insulation, leaving a small entrance, next to which was an open area for a fire.

I let myself linger a while, and imagine *il y a 6000 ans*. In that isolation I began to hear the forest noises, the sounds of the birds, and some unidentifiable animals. A snapping twig might be an approaching predator, I thought, my adrenaline pumping. With my imagination racing, I could understand—could *sense*—how each day of life six thousand years ago was consumed with the search for food, how the need to maintain a fire was a matter of life-and-death, how the blackness of night could bring such terrors, and how the rising sun could seem like a god. Touching those stones sent a shiver through me as I thought of the nameless humans who built this dolmen and of the miracle of their survival.

I continued on the path and crossed a stream that created a marshy area where heavy vines dangled from the tree limbs. Here the path had been fitted with a sort of boardwalk so the hiker might avoid stepping in the mud. I was reminded that this trail was part of an extensive recreational area and that Méjannes-le-Clap had housing for youth groups, with swimming pools, tennis courts, and horse stables. Why I was lucky enough to be the only soul around was a mystery, for it was a fine day. Almost by accident I stumbled upon the second dolmen in the area, this one without a descriptive placard with the approximate age. I thought it looked somewhat less well-situated, smaller, and with large gaps between the huge stones that I thought would be more difficult to fill with dirt and sod. I supposed there was a large variation in the style and construction of these prehistoric shelters, each representing the particular needs of the builders. I considered how, several hundred kilometers north of here, was the city of Paris, so famous for its exquisite architecture, and here I was standing before this rough dwelling, an example of man's earliest architecture.

The afternoon sun was getting low in the sky, and my desire for experiencing prehistoric life did not include a night alone in the forest. I trudged back to the car feeling grateful for civilization. How fortunate I was to be able to return to the comfortable house in the village, secure behind locked doors, with electric lights, plenty of good food, a warm bed, and hot and cold running water!

CHAPTER 4

On Language

Linguistic Faux Pas— How English became English — Why Do the French Speak French and the Germans Speak German? — The Conversion of Clovis

I am constantly amused and delighted at how often I am mistaken for French. Is it possible that I might actually seem to fit in here? For example, one morning I was sweeping the courtyard steps outside the garden wall when an American couple wandered down the path from the château. We exchanged *bonjours*, and then the lady politely complimented the village by commenting, "*C'est un très joli village.*" (it is a very pretty village) I agreed "*Oui, Madame, c'est vrai,*" (it is true) and asked, "*Vous parlez anglais?*" exposing my act. It turned out they were from Iowa and were staying near Uzès, having spent a week in Paris. They told me they were having a wonderful time, but they were surprised how few people in *le Midi* spoke English. They were also surprised to find an American in this tiny village. The gentleman couldn't help asking whether living here was difficult and where I bought my groceries. I told them a little

The valley at dawn

of my adjustments here, assured them I was managing nicely, and wished them a pleasant stay and safe trip home.

Another time, while sitting in my car at the stoplight at the Charles Martel Bridge, I overheard a family of British tourists wondering about the distance to the *Cascades de Sautedet*. I wasn't used to hearing English spoken in the village, so to be helpful and friendly, I gestured to the right, smiling. The gentleman, assuming I was French, said, "*Merci, Madame,*" and asked how far. I replied, "About a five-minute walk," and he remarked, "What beautiful English." I chuckled to think that if he had known I was American, he wouldn't have thought I spoke beautiful English! But to be pleasant, I said, "My French is not beautiful." Now quite startled, he asked me where I was from, and I said, "Chicago" with a grin just as the light changed. So, stepping on the gas, I made a theatrical exit, waving good-bye and wishing them a great holiday. Leave 'em laughing, I always say.

Driving through the countryside, I realized how glad I was to have English as my first language. With my struggles to learn French, I might never have been able to learn English with its massive vocabulary if it had not been my mother tongue. Not that French is that much simpler to learn than English; it's just difficult in different ways.

My efforts to learn to speak French have become a long-running gag in my family, with my nearest and dearest comparing my repeated French 101 classes with the Red Cross's numerous failures to teach me to swim. But, I would protest, French is a complex and subtle language, full of strange idioms, exceptions to the complicated grammatical rules, a long list of irregular verbs, unfamiliar sentence structure, and silent final consonants. My usual experience while travelling and attempting to converse with a French native was, after struggling to construct and pronounce a question, to have it met with a rapid-fire string of vowel sounds in reply, producing in me the classic deer-in-the-headlights look. If ever the day dawned when I found myself even moderately competent in French, I might write an essay inspired by Mark Twain's "Horrors of the German Language" and call it "On the Terrors of the French Language."

❱ ❰

Context is so important in comprehension, especially when trying to grasp the gist of a conversation in the French language, because French has so many homonyms (words that sound the same but have different meanings). But really, context is important in understanding any foreign language. I remember an episode early in our travels together when my daughter and I were touring Italy. For that vacation we rented a small car for seeing the country-side, which did expand our impressions of the Italian experience. In fact, we found the people in the small villages to be warm and friendly. We had stopped in one lovely little Tuscan village over a weekend and decided to attend Sunday Mass at the ancient church. We entered the stone vestibule and were greeted by the middle-aged church ladies—easily recognizable types, no matter what country you are in. After we selected our seats, one of the church ladies approached us with a smile and whispered something unintelligible to me, gesturing to the small missal Kate had picked up at the church entrance.

"What was that all about?" I whispered to Kate when the lady left.

"I think she was just showing us where the Mass liturgy for today was in the missal."

"Oh, okay."

When the time came for the readings from the Old Testament, a member of the congregation went to the lectern and did the reading, followed by Psalms, all in Italian, naturally. When it was time for the second reading, there was an uncomfortable pause, and then the entire congregation turned in unison to look at us. "Holy s--t!" I nearly blurted. That lady had asked *me* to do the reading! In my almost nonexistent Italian? Trapped, I turned to Kate, who was just as confused as to what to do.

"*Pssst, Signora, prego!*" I gestured frantically to the church lady to come over to me, but I was so embarrassed I could hardly explain. However, she was gracious enough to understand. She gathered up her dignity, marched to the lectern, and gave the reading beautifully. As my pulse rate returned to normal, I glanced at Kate, who stole a glance at me. We both burst into uncontrollable giggles, which we failed to suppress and rocked the bench we were sitting on. I'm sure the motion could be felt by the people around us.

Leaving the church, we were again greeted by *buongiornos,* but with a hint of smiles of amusement at our silly behavior. No approbation, just friendliness. I was much relieved.

I realized later that I should have recognized what that lady was asking. If I only had been alert to the context, the situation in which she was asking—that is, inviting me as a visitor to do the reading for the Mass—I could have politely declined. Oh well. Another embarrassing foreign language moment.

༄ ༄

But how did the French language develop? In *The History of the Franks* by the sixth-century historian Gregory, Bishop of Tours, who lived from 539 to 594 and was the author of many books of church and civil history in France of the Late Antiquity, Gregory describes the Frankish people, the ancestors of the French, who were originally German. But if the Franks, the third-century confederation of old German tribes of Free Germany who migrated into Gaul in the fourth century, had similar origins and customs of the other Teutonic tribes, how did they come to create the French identity and develop the French language? If the Germans and French both claim descent from Charlemagne, and, as we were taught in school, if the Frankish Kingdom is the antecedent for both the German nation and the French nation, why do the Germans speak German and the French speak French?

We know the story of how modern English developed. When my daughter and I first travelled through England many years ago, we visited the site of the Battle of Hastings—that great battle fought in October 1066 between William, Duke of Normandy, and Harold, the last Saxon King of England. I remember walking over the battlefield, standing on the ridge where the Saxon army had assembled, looking down the gentle slope to the marshy lowlands that had to be crossed by the Norman cavalry and infantry, and imagining wave after wave of attacks. I walked over the foundation stones that were all that was left of the church built by William years after the battle to atone for causing Harold's death. William had the altar set on the place where tradition says Harold fell, pierced through the eye by an arrow. On a wall near the church ruins, I found a stone plaque that stated: "This stone has been set in this place to commemorate the fusion of the English and Norman Peoples which resulted from the Great Battle fought here in 1066." A shiver of recognition ran down my back; this was the birthplace of a mighty language.

Because of his victory that day, Duke William of Normandy became King William I of England, anointed and crowned at Westminster Abbey on Christmas Day, 1066. What followed over the next few decades was nothing short of a complete takeover by William and his Norman barons of the land and wealth of the Saxon aristocracy, a story made famous in the Robin Hood and Ivanhoe epics. To maintain power and ensure control of his conquered kingdom and the loyalty of his subjects, King William replaced the Saxon churchmen with Norman bishops, created great Norman landowners from the confiscated Saxon estates, and filled the royal court with his Norman French-speaking officials. For the next 250, years there existed one kingdom with two languages, the Norman French of the aristocratic landowners and the Anglo-Saxon Old English of the peasantry. The kings of England spoke Norman French at court through the reign of Edward III in the mid-1300s. This helps explain why the motto of the Order of the Garter, which Edward established in 1348, and as spoken by Edward, is in French: *Honi soit qui mal y pense:* Shame to him who thinks ill of it. I remember studying *Macbeth* in high school and finding a great example of how Shakespeare managed to cater to an audience of different linguistic backgrounds. In Act II, scene 2, lines 54–60, Macbeth laments, "…will all great Neptune's ocean wash this blood clean from my hand? No, this my hand will rather the multitudinous seas incarnadine, making the green one red." It was as if Shakespeare couldn't resist inserting a nifty Latin-French neologism "incarnadine," meaning to turn red, for his upper-class patrons, and yet restated the word in Anglo-Saxon terms accessible to those in the penny seats. I've read how English has the largest vocabulary of modern languages, and it is easy to believe because it represents the combination of the vocabularies of both the Old English Anglo-Saxon German and Norman French, with other contributors such as Latin, Greek, and Scandinavian languages thrown in. Modern English is filled with synonyms with medieval French and English antecedents; for example, Old English "cow," "sheep," and "pig" and Old French *boeuf, mouton,* and *porc,* which presumes to indicate the social status of the speaker—the Saxon peasant who cared for the animals and the Norman French aristocrat who ate the prepared meat.

∽ ∼

The Battle of Hastings can be used to date the creation of Modern English, making it unique among European languages. While French might not have such a signpost event in its history, linguistic scholars can give fairly accurate boundary limits on the chronological development of the French language, starting from the Roman invasion. Clearly, the evolution of Latin into French is a result of the five hundred years of Roman dominance in Gaul. The Romans introduced Latin to the Gallic Celts when Julius Caesar conquered them in a series of battles from 59 to 49 BC and stationed his Legions throughout Gaul. With the successful military subjugation of Celtic Gaul and the establishment of Roman Provence, the stage was set for the assimilation of the Gallic peoples into the Roman way of life, *Romanitas*. The Gallic aristocrats were encouraged to assume Roman culture, religion, and language, along with the Roman legal system. Thus began the Gallo-Roman hybrid culture. The Gallic Celts must have been sharp; they quickly recognized the advantages of Roman organization and cultural improvements to their lifestyle. Their *oppida* grew into cities, trade and commerce was enhanced and profitable, the Gallic aristocracy was given Roman administrative duties and eventual Roman citizenship, and Latin became the language for literature, law, and correspondence. For five hundred years, Latin was merged with the Celtic language, which did not exist in a written form, producing a Gallo-Roman vernacular called Vulgar Latin (but not that kind of vulgar), recognizable by the sixth century AD, and was the language of Gregory of Tours. Vulgar Latin was likely a language spoken by Charlemagne, although his mother tongue was probably Frankish, the old Germanic language.

In 842 AD, the Oaths of Strasbourg were proclaimed by two of Charlemagne's grandsons in the presence of their combined armies, in an attempt to form an alliance against a third grandson. To ensure the followers of both brothers understood what was being pledged, each brother swore the oath in the language of the other. Louis the German, king of the East Franks, read the oath in Vulgar Latin, and Charles the Bald, king of the West Franks, read the oath in Old German. The text of the Strasbourg Oath has been called the earliest example of Vulgar Latin, which became Old French and then modern French. The text of the oath also provides an example of Old German, which became modern German.

The Frankish Kingdom, which eventually replaced Roman control in Gaul, became the nucleus of the future nations of France and Germany. In addition, what later became the Kingdom of France and Reich of Germany both traced their lineage back to the Empire of Charlemagne. The infamous Third Reich of Adolf Hitler was so called to confer on it a noble pedigree descending from the First Reich of Charlemagne and the Second Reich of Kaiser Wilhelm I in 1871, when more than two dozen independent states from the old Holy Roman Empire were united with Prussia to create the German Empire. In tracing the history and evolution of both France and Germany, we find the paths dovetail and merge into the history of the Frankish Kingdom. The Germans and French share a Frankish heritage and history, but not language. One could argue that the historical animosity between France and Germany is traceable to the Oaths of Strasbourg, when the Frankish tribes sought to define their eastern and western spheres of influence, and by doing so, codified their separate and distinct peoples. But how and why did the languages of the Frankish tribes split into German and French? This question has haunted me during my travels through Provence and my visits to Germany.

After hours of contemplation lubricated by multiple glasses of wine, I hit upon a scenario, my own personal hypotheses! Clearly, I reasoned, the text of the Oaths of Strasbourg indicates that by

842 the East Franks spoke an early German and the West Franks spoke an early French based on Vulgar Latin. Thus, the chronological boundary limits on the development of Vulgar Latin into early French are from roughly the first century through the ninth century, by which time Old French and Old German were separate and distinct. It is possible that the East Franks and the West Franks had separated linguistically much earlier, perhaps as early as the fifth century, and certainly by the sixth. After all, we have the Histories of Gregory of Tours, who wrote in recognizable Vulgar Latin in the late sixth century. So I started thinking of the factors at work prior to the sixth century AD that might have contributed to that language bifurcation.

For the first three centuries AD, Rome controlled the land of the Gauls and offered *Romanitas* to the German barbaric tribes across the frontiers. Not all barbarians were so willing to ally with Rome. The intentions of the migrating Ostrogoths and Visigoths seemed to have been adversarial and rapacious, as demonstrated in the eventual Sack of Rome in 410 AD by the Visigoths led by Alarac I. The Franks, however, seemed to have had a high regard for Roman culture and were more willing to coexist peaceably with their Gallo-Roman neighbors in Gaul. Unlike the other Germanic tribes who crossed the frontier of the Roman Empire during the Great Migration of the fourth century, the Franks felt an admiration for the Roman way of life and for all things appertaining to Rome. This seems to be an important and crucial distinction in the subsequent development of the French language.

According to the scholarly works of Peter Brown in *The World of Late Antiquity* and Patrick J. Geary in *Before France and Germany*, the Frankish tribes who gradually overtook control of Gaul merged with the indigenous Gallo-Romans, blending their cultures, social structures, and legal systems. The two languages, the Old Frankish Germanic dialect and the Vulgar Latin of the

Gallo-Romans, must have existed side by side for years, but the Frankish language did not supplant the Latin, as sometimes happens to a conquered people. The other Germanic tribes who overran eastern Roman territory—for example, the Saxons and Bavarians—kept their native speech, and Vulgar Latin gradually disappeared from the territory later called the East Frankish Kingdom of Louis the German. Why were the West Franks under King Charles the Bald different?

If there is an answer, I think it could date back some 350 years before the Oaths of Strasbourg and may be due to the life and leadership of a remarkable man, Clovis I, the Merovingian king of the Franks. Clovis (circa 465–511), the grandson of the shadowy Frankish leader Merovech, rose to power and prominence in 486 by defeating the last Roman magistrate in Gaul, Syagrius, for control of *Belgae Secunda*, northeastern France around what is now Paris. According to Gregory of Tours, Clovis solidified his control over his Salian Franks by eliminating any kinsmen who might compete with him for power. In 493 the still-pagan Clovis married Clotilde, the Burgundian princess who, interestingly for my hypothesis, was an Orthodox Christian of the Roman rite, instead of an Arian Christian like her Burgundian kinsmen.

The Arian-Orthodox Christianity controversy was an enormously destabilizing force in the history of the early Christian Church. Considered a heresy, Arianism was named for Bishop Arius (260–336) of Alexandria in Egypt who preached that Christ was not of the same substance as God, therefore not equal with God, and was thus not truly divine, but a created being. Arius denied the concept of the Trinity—the Father, the Son and the Holy Ghost—teaching the uniqueness of God alone. According to Arius's opponents, especially Bishop Athanasius of Alexandria, who was called the father of Orthodoxy, Arius's teaching reduced the Son to the status of a demigod, potentially reintroducing polytheism and undermining the Christian concept of redemption. For many years the controversy raged between the Arian Christians and the Orthodox Roman Christians. This controversy seemed to be brought to an end at the Council of Nicaea, assembled by the Emperor Constantine in 325 AD, which condemned Arius and his teachings. The council introduced the Nicene Creed — with the word *filioque*, from the Son, to proclaim the Son to be one substance with the Father — into the *Credo*. The Nicene Creed is still used today in the Roman Catholic Mass. Nevertheless, the Arian Heresy persisted until the seventh century and was the source of long-standing disputes. Gregory of Tours spent many pages in the *History of the Franks* arguing against Arianism and defending Orthodoxy.

Hundreds of years before Gregory was bishop of Tours and wrote his histories, the Arian form of Christianity was brought to the Gothic and Vandal tribes east of the Rhine, outside the Roman Empire, in about 370 AD by Ulfilas, who was a disciple of Arius. In his efforts to establish Arian Christianity among the pagan and unlettered Goths, Ulfilas created a Gothic alphabet using Greek letters and translated the Bible from Greek into Gothic. The truly monumental linguistic work by Ulfilas resulted in huge numbers of Visigothics and Ostrogothics converting from paganism to Arian Christianity. Also converted to Arian Christianity were Saxon and Bavarian populations who lived outside the Roman frontier east of the Rhine River, long before the end of the Western Roman Empire in 476. When the Great Migrations began, the Gothic tribes carried Arianism with them into what became Visigothic Spain and Ostrogothic Italy. The introduction of Arianism to the Goths led to years of conflict with and separation from the indigenous Orthodox Roman Christians. The situation may be contrasted with that of the Franks, who migrated from Germany into Gaul as pagans, lived side by side with the Gallo-Romans, and were converted directly to Orthodox Roman Christianity through the leadership of Clovis, the King of the Franks.

Gregory of Tours describes the Conversion of Clovis as having been instigated by his Orthodox Christian wife, Clotilde, who insisted on having their infant son baptized. When the child died, Clovis blamed the baptism and told her the baby should have been dedicated to the pagan gods. But Clotilde persisted and again persuaded Clovis to have their next child baptized, insisting that the pagan gods were powerless. Gregory relates the story of how Clovis, when in a fierce battle against the Alemanni at Tolbiac in 496, called on Clotilde's Christian God for help. He pledged to be baptized if victorious, an episode that can only be called a retelling of the Conversion of the Roman Emperor Constantine during the Battle of Malvian Bridge in 312 AD.

But the crucial factor was the Orthodox Christianity of Clotilde, who insisted and directed Clovis to be baptized Orthodox, not Arian, in 496. As was the custom then, and because it was standard practice for the people ruled to follow the same religious beliefs as their rulers, all of Clovis's retinue, vassals, and armies were also baptized, some three thousand in number, according to Gregory of Tours. The significance is enormous; had Clovis and his Franks become Arians, they would have remained closely allied with the German-speaking Gothic Arians and, consequently, may have retained their Germanic Frankish language. But the acceptance into the Roman rites of Christianity confirmed the Franks' acceptance of *Romanitas* and proclaimed their close alliance with the Latin-speaking Gallo-Romans of Gaul as well as identification with the power and prestige of what was left of the Western Roman Empire. No religious barrier separated the Frankish people from the Gallo-Romans. It was as if, with the Conversion of Clovis, the Frankish people and the Gallo-Romans amalgamated and developed what became a separate and distinct

French culture and language as the inheritors of Ancient Rome. With that one decision, Clovis directed a new chapter for Western Civilization.

As a result of Clovis's leadership and his conversion from paganism, the Franks established separate and independent control of their remnant of the Gallo-Roman territory. And in embracing Orthodox Christianity, they set themselves up as heirs of the Roman traditions. They also established themselves as the defenders of the pope and the true faith, which justified the task of conquering and converting the heretics and bringing the land of the heretics under Frankish control. In his *History of the Franks*, Book II, Gregory records Clovis as stating, "I find it hard to see these Arians as occupying part of Gaul. With God's help let us invade them. When we have beaten them, we will take over their territory." The Franks inherited Roman economic and legal structures, as well as the network of Roman roads, towns, and commercial systems. They also maintained the methods of Roman government organization, administration, and bureaucracy.

In contrast, the Visigothic Kingdom in Provence of Alaric II promulgated laws against the assimilation of Gothic Arians and Gallo-Roman Christians, and generally they maintained separate communities with separate churches and clergy. This separation probably led to the cultures maintaining their separate languages, Gothic and Vulgar Latin. Similarly, in the Ostrogothic Kingdom of northern Italy, Professor Geary suggests the Ostrogothic king Theodoric failed to establish a dynasty because in promoting the separation between his Arian and Orthodox people, he never permitted a synthesis of Roman and Gothic societies. This ultimately destabilized his Ostrogothic nation, opening the door for the Langobard invasion in 568.

The Franks were quite successful in their campaign to conquer and convert the Arian Kingdoms of the Visigoths and Ostrogoths.

Clovis and his Merovingian successors gradually brought more and more territory under Frankish control, which grew to encompass most of Western Europe during the Empire of Charlemagne. The Langobards brought an end to the Arian Ostrogothic Kingdom in Italy, and in 789 Charlemagne conquered the Langobards, restoring Roman Christianity to northern Italy. The Visigothic lands in Provence were conquered by the Franks in the sixth century, and in 586 Visigothic King Reccared I of Spain converted to Orthodox Christianity, bringing an end to the Arian heresy in Visigothic Spain. Arianism gradually faded from history after the seventh century, by which time the linguistic separation between Old German speakers and Old French speakers probably had long been culturally established.

So my hypothesis of why the French speak a Latin-based language while their German cousins continue to use German hinges on the acceptance by the Franks of the Roman Christian religion instead of the Arianism of the Goths. Not wishing to believe that I had come upon this idea independently—because there is nothing new under the sun—I searched through every book on early French and German history that I could find. Perhaps my searches were misdirected because I came up empty. However, during my days of exploring in southern France, I was able to spend some time at the Regional Archives of Gard at Nîmes, a fantastic research center for the Gard Department. During my search through the archives for information on the evolution of the French language, I found some supporting statements in an old encyclopedia called the *Histoire Generale de Languedoc* in an article dating from 1872. The Benedictine scholars who compiled this encyclopedia wrote an essay on the *"Usage des langues grecque et latine conserré dans la Province"* the conservation of the usage of the Greek and Latin languages in Provence, with a paragraph suggesting the Arian Visigoths of Provence maintained a separate society from the ancient *catholique* people of Provence because of their different religions. This separation contributed to the conservation of the usage of Latin in what is now Languedoc and Provence, as well as the other provinces of Gaul. Thus, the Benedictine scholars conclude, the long-running controversy between Arianism and Roman Christianity was the *repelling* force that kept the Vulgar Latin-speaking Frankish people separate from the German-speaking Arians and permitted the Franks sufficient isolation to evolve their Vulgar Latin into the Old French of the Oath of Strasbourg.

I was thrilled with the discovery of this document, which I boldly interpreted as supporting my own hypothesis. Evidently I was not the only person travelling through these lands who had explored the reasons for the separation of the French and German languages; the very same question had been considered and addressed by these nineteenth-century Benedictine scholars. Of course, one source does not a proof make, but I felt more comfortable knowing that I was not alone in trying to figure out the possible historical connections that impelled the Germanic Franks to give up their Germanic language and adopt Vulgar Latin, leading to the development of the modern French language. It is possible that the development of the French language might be connected to the seemingly unrelated event called the Conversion of Clovis.

CHAPTER 5

The Romans Were Everywhere!

Visit to Orange and Vaison-la-Romaine — Search for the Camp du César — Julius Caesar

The weather had been somewhat unsettled—windy days with a few clouds changing to cooler, overcast days with some sprinkles of rain. But this morning was picture perfect. I spent the coolness of the hours after sunrise on the kitchen terrace, just watching the wind rolling across the wooded hillsides and the birds riding the thermals. I spotted two grey hawks in the distance, wings outstretched, gliding on the warm air currents, and a wave of utter serenity passed over me. The hawks circled each other, bright in the sunlight, framed against the dark, misty green of the forest they soared above. They seemed to be heading toward the village, crossing over the St. Laurent vineyards and the Cèze River until they were quite close. Sitting on the kitchen terrace, I was just about at eye level with the swooping skylarks, swallows, and pigeons, but had not seen such large birds as those hawks. I watched them until they gracefully circled themselves past the west ridge of the mountain and disappeared.

Watching the trees on the hillsides bend against the wind, I could imagine how the ancient inhabitants of these lands explained the wind as being controlled by the gods. One could be persuaded to believe a giant, unseen hand was moving along the rim of the hill, mashing down the tree tops as it progressed. Certainly not a scientific explanation, but it is hardly less satisfying a description.

❧ ❧

If one were to ask what were the most lasting influences in the history and development of southern France, one safe answer would be the Romans. The Romans were everywhere.

The standard tours of this region usually include the city of Orange, which has two amazing Roman buildings, the Roman Theatre and Arc de Triomphe, both of which are UNESCO World Heritage Sites. During our vacation in La Gorce in 2005, Marc and Kate took me to Orange to give me a taste of the ancient wonders to discover and to visit the Arc de Triomphe and the Roman Theatre. The city, originally called *Arausio*, started as a Celtic settlement and prospered under the Romans. A horrible battle took place here in 105 BC when the Romans suffered a defeat against the invading German tribes of Cimbri and Teutons, but the Romans recovered from the disaster to establish *Arausio*, and they subsequently built temples, baths, a circus, a commemorative arch, and a theatre, of which only the last two survived the Middle Ages. The arch served as a city gate on what was the Via Agrippa, the road which dates from 39 BC, built by Augustus's general Agrippa that linked Arles and Lyon. The arch's design reminded me of the Arch of Constantine in Rome, and I read later that this may have been an early model. That this arch made it intact through the centuries, when so many other Roman buildings were used as stone quarries for medieval builders, is a miracle.

The theatre in particular is a marvel; no other Roman theatre, in or out of Italy, has survived with its original stage wall intact. I read how, after a visit to Orange, King Louis XIV proclaimed the theatre wall to be the most beautiful wall in the French kingdom—quite a statement from the man who built Versailles. The theatre could hold eleven thousand spectators, and in its restored state still accommodates seven thousand for operatic or dramatic performances. Today the theatre is home to a famous music festival, thanks to the still-fantastic acoustics. When we toured the interior, I was fascinated to see a huge statue of the Emperor Augustus in a niche above the center stage wall. Next to the theatre we saw the remains of what was a gymnasium complete with small temples, running tracks, and an area for wrestling matches, all undergoing excavation and conservation. Like so many other cities in Roman Gaul, the city of Orange suffered years of destruction and war under the control of successive rulers such as the kings of Burgundy, the lords of Beaux, and the princes of Orange. When William the Silent, the prince of Orange-Nassau, became governor of the United Provinces of the Low Countries in 1544, the name Orange became bound forever to the Dutch royalty, with far-reaching connections in European history.

∽ ∾

That following summer, when I first stayed in the village with Kate, I persuaded her to give up a day of cycling the hills up to Barjac, and drive with me to visit the town of Vaison-la-Romaine and the ancient Roman ruins. I had read that Vaison contained the most extensive Roman city ruins in the South of France, and I was eager to explore. The drive took us almost due east, across rolling farmlands and vineyards simmering in the warm summer morning, to the modern village of Vaison on the Ouvèze River at the base of Mont

Ventoux. We found the car park and paid the entrance fee, and soon were strolling through the ancient streets. The placards explained how Vaison had been the capital of the Celtic tribe, the Voconzi, in the fourth century BC and was renamed Vasio Vocontiorum by the Romans. When Vasio was elevated to a *civitas foederata*, a city allied with Rome, that privilege brought wealth, prestige, political advantages, and fine buildings, including a forum, theatre, basilica, merchants' villas, and baths—all richly decorated with mosaic floors and sculptures. We walked through the Portico of Pompey, a large public meeting-place built around a garden. One could see evidence of frescoes on the walls and view the niches that held copies of larger-than-life statues of the Emperor Hadrian, his wife, Sabina, and the famous ancient sculptor Polycletus', *Diadumenos*, (The original statues of Hadrian and Sabina are in the Vaison Museum; the original statue of *Diadumenos* is in the British Museum in London.) We stopped in the museum to get out of the intense heat and found a wealth of antiquities from the site, including the marble wreathed head of Apollo, theatre masks, and floor mosaics. Everyday objects included oil lamps, kitchen utensils, and a small terracotta votive sculpture of a roofed shrine containing three seated figures badly eroded, representing the Matres, female deities of the Gallo-Romans. What a fascinating glimpse of first century AD life in Vaison.

Vaison-la-Romaine fell into decline with the warring Ostrogoths and Burgundians, and for safety, the medieval inhabitants moved closer to a castle built on the rocky outcrop above the river, leaving the Roman city to crumble. In the eighteenth century, the people moved back to the lower site near the river and built the present city over the ancient Vasio. Thus, much of the Roman city lies under the modern city and remains frustratingly unexplored.

❧ ❧

Tower and ramparts on *Camp du César*

The Romans were everywhere. Now that I was here on my own, I wanted to see as much of Roman Provence as I could. Using the visitor's brochures from the *Maison de Patrimonie et Histoire*, I chose as my first Roman destination the Gallic *oppidum* and Roman military post called *Le Camp du César*. I set out early one morning for the lovely stone village of Laudun, about fifteen kilometers south of our village. Once in the town, I realized that the directions to the Roman site were not as large and obvious as I had expected them to be, and after driving in circles for almost an hour, I nearly turned back discouraged. Apparently, this Roman site is not the main attraction for Laudun, as opposed to cities such as Orange or Nîmes or Vaison-la-Romaine, which boast of their Roman pasts with numerous road signs guiding the tourists. At last I found the right road with rustic signs pointing to the Camp du César on a hill above the town and continued on. The paved road became a small dirt lane, twisting and climbing upward until I reached the car park. I got out and hiked the rest of the way.

I was glad I had persevered. What a treat! I had the place almost all to myself. Approaching on foot with the village of Laudun below, I found the Camp du César was a sort of plateau above the Rhône River Valley. The first thing I saw when I arrived was the huge round stone tower, the best-preserved Roman tower in the South of France, with the remnants of the Roman fortifications and public buildings in an orderly arrangement. The camp covered about eighteen hectares (about forty-five acres), and one could see immediately why the location was chosen: It was a perfect lookout with the Rhône clearly visible in the distance, and any activity along the valley could be easily spotted by a sentry. Of course the Gallic *oppidum* was built for defensive purposes, and I should have remembered that the highest terrain in the area would have been chosen for such a camp.

This plateau had been in use by Gallic tribes since the fifth century BC, and the *oppidum* they built had been taken over by the Romans in the first century BC. As I strolled over the camp, I allowed myself to try to pick out the ramparts that were built by the Gauls and those built by the Romans. Helpful placards were posted at various spots to identify the ruins. The Gallic walls with the rough, uneven stones and crude construction contrasted with the more sophisticated Roman smooth-stone building technique, something like comparing prairie sod houses with brick-and-mortar construction in the American Old West. The Romans built extensively here; one could clearly see the remains of the basilica, the forum, the arsenal, and the legionnaires' living quarters, as well as the amazing ten-meter-high tower built into the sturdy stone wall surrounding the site, all displaying sound engineering and architectural planning. Clearly, the Romans built to last. Walking across the open space near the storehouses, I found the placard identifying the former location of stables, and I could almost smell the horses. I wondered what the source of water was. Remembering the Romans' love of fresh water, I figured there must have been a cistern for collecting rainwater, but I couldn't find one, and no one was around to ask where it might be.

The camp was in use until the sixth century AD and then was abandoned during the transition from Gallo-Roman control to the Visigothic kings. That the camp is unused may be true, but I noticed a military-looking truck parked nearby in the shade of a clump of trees. Curious, I wandered up a small path to the highest part of the plateau and discovered a modern military camp, clearly occupied with a pitched tent, bundles of supplies, communications gear, and a French soldier napping on a cot, a wine bottle next to his boots. I left quietly, thinking how that scene had merged the past with the present.

The sunlight was fading into late afternoon, and I was getting hungry. Reluctantly, I walked down to the car and started the journey home. Driving back to the village, I considered it strange that the Roman camp did not have that ancient feel to it at all. I had not experienced the sensation of stepping back in time. I wondered whether other Roman sites I found might give that sensation of the passage of two thousand years. Later in the evening, curled up on the sofa with my books and music, I started to plan my next excursion. As I did so, I let my mind wander over what I had explored at the Camp du César and read about the string of connections that brought the Romans to Provence.

∽ ∾

After the Celtic tribes of the Late Bronze Age (1300–800 BC) established themselves and developed settlements in Southern Europe and on the Italian Peninsula, they began setting up contacts with the Mycenaean Greek traders from the Aegean city-states. There is archaeological evidence of bronze goods, pottery, and glass from Bronze Age Greek workshops turning up in southern France. Greek trade routes stretched east from the Black Sea to the western Mediterranean, and around 600 BC the port of Massalia, modern Marseilles, was set up by the Greek colonists for trade with tribes they called *keltoi*, identified by the Romans as Gauls, along the upper Rhône River.

The Greeks were not the empire-builders, but rather the emporium-builders. They were interested not in conquest but in new markets for their products in exchange for Gallic furs, grain, and metals. This trade also provided the mechanism for the spread of the Greek culture and civilization into the barbaric hinterland of Gaul. To the Greeks, anyone who could not speak Greek was a barbarian, and they sought to teach the barbarians their culture and language. Many social factors, including wars, famine, and overpopulation, led to the need for the Greeks to colonize in the regions of the Mediterranean. The development of new crafts called for expanded trade; population surpluses and social conflicts drove people to extend their boundaries. The Greek cities in Ionia became the mother of many urban settlements on the Black Sea, the southwest coast of Italy, and southern France from Massalia (Marseille) in 600 BC to Nicaea (Nice) in 550 BC. The Greeks trained the Gauls in defending their property and holdings by building *oppida*. Some of the old settlements gradually became new trading posts, which needed to be fortified against raiders, hence the development of *oppida*, of which the Camp du César surely started out as in its Gallic phase.

The death of Alexander the Great in 323 BC ended the expansion of the Greek colonies and their territorial control. Alexander's empire was split among his generals, and control of the rustic western Mediterranean was not deemed valuable enough for his generals, who preferred to concentrate on the highly civilized, cultured, and wealthy cities of the Middle East and Egypt. So control of the western colonies passed by default back into the hands of the local Gallic tribes.

How did the Romans get involved with this? After all, trade had been the purview of the Greeks and also involved the Etruscans, who were the major power in Italy and had a well-developed Bronze Age culture, identified by archaeologists as Villanovan. The Bronze Age Greeks would have barely noticed the rustic Romans in Italy, and rustic they were in 600 BC. The dominant civilization belonged to the Etruscans, who held the power on the Italian peninsula. The origins of Rome have been traced to the Latinii, an insignificant tribe within the Etruscan Confederacy in the sixth century BC. There were many such tribes then: the Veneti on the Po River, the Ligurians around the Gulf of Genoa, the Umbrians in the land east of the Tiber River, and the cluster of the tribes to the south, the Sabines, the Samnites, and the Osci. The Latinii were just another obscure and simple farming people with little to distinguish them from the other Italic people under the control of the Etruscans. However, within a few centuries, the descendants of the Latinii were to become masters of the Western world.

How the Romans pulled themselves together, threw off the Etruscan kings, and developed into the greatest empire of Western antiquity is the subject of many scholarly works and a fascinating story. At its greatest extent in 117 AD under the rule of the Emperor Trajan, the Roman Empire stretched from the Caspian Sea and the Persian Gulf in the east, south to Egypt, across the North African desert west to Morocco, across Europe from Spain to the eastern borders on the Rhine and Danube, and to the north of England. I remember on a trip to England visiting Hadrian's Wall in Northumbria with the thrill of realizing I was at the northernmost extent of the Roman Empire and knowing I was a long way from Rome.

But at the start of the first century BC, Rome was still a republic, and the Romans were focused on the wars with Carthage, Rome's competitor for power in the Mediterranean. The Romans called the Mediterranean *mare nostrum*, our sea, and knew their power, freedom, wealth, and security depended on controlling the sea. Much of the cause of Roman expansion, colonization, and occupation can be explained by their obsessive need to control the Mediterranean. Like the rest of the east, they were largely unconcerned with the trade cities of the Rhône delta. However, the lucrative trading and the profits to be gained fueled the interest of invading tribes from the north called the Salyans. People then, as now, fought fiercely for control of the land and economic wealth attached to it. In 125 BC the citizens of Massalia appealed to Rome for protection from these encroaching Salyans, who had set up an *oppidum* at Entremont.

The citizens' request resulted in the arrival of Roman Legions. Thus began the period of Roman colonization.

Answering the appeal in 122 BC, the Roman Proconsul Caius Sextius Calvinius and his legions overcame the Salyans at Entrement and took control of the city, which they named *Aquae Sextia Salluvoirum* because of the thermal springs nearby. This was the foundation of the modern city of Aix-en-Provence. In 102 BC the troops of the Roman general Gaius Marius defeated the barbarian Cimbrian and Teutonic raiding parties, the same tribes that had defeated the Romans at Aurosio three years before, one of many incursions into the region. In 61 BC the whole of Provence was put under Roman protection as the first province outside of Italy. The Romans stayed for another five hundred years.

I find it interesting to consider other cases in history where the appeal by a besieged people to powerful overlords for temporary protection ends up as long-term occupation and control. For example, the English under Henry II came to Ireland in 1171 at the behest of Diarmait MacMurchada of Leinster, who was losing his battle for power against the High King of Ireland and needed help. Henry's Norman troops invaded and subdued the king, and Ireland fell under the control of England for the next eight hundred years. There are many other instances, and they serve to reinforce the warning "be careful what you ask for."

When the Romans subdued the Gallic Celts and established their protectorate, they called the region Gallia Narbonensis after the Roman city of Narbonensis, or Provincia, as the first province. Much of what we know about these Gallic-Celtic people comes from the writings of Julius Caesar, probably one of the most famous names in world history. In my father's generation, Latin was a common subject in high school, and my dad still remembers the opening phrase in Caesar's *Commentaries of the Gallic Wars*: "*Gallia est omnis divisa in partes tres...*" translated as "Gaul is as a whole divided into three parts." What followed was Caesar's multivolume eyewitness account of the wars with astute observations on the Gallic people and their way of life.

I believe Julius Caesar's character has been much maligned in recent times. Reviewing the life of Caesar in detail, one can see how deserving he is of lasting fame as a politician and statesman, as well as a military general and historian. Gaius Julius Caesar was born into a Roman aristocratic family—*gens Julii*—around 100 BC and was drawn into politics. We first read of him in 60 BC as one of the Triumvirate, along with Pompey and Crassus—of *Spartacus* fame— that jointly led the government. At that time Rome was a republic with the controlling aristocratic Patrician party in the Senate spending much time and effort suppressing the Plebian political factions of commoners. Because Julius Caesar favored the Plebian political representation, he made enemies among the aristocrats in the Senate. He served a one-year term as Roman consul. When his elected term was over, the Senate, fearing his popularity with the people, sent him to Gaul to become governor. At about this time, around 59 BC, the Celtic tribe called Helvetians, living in what is now Switzerland, started a mass migration west. To have thousands of people on the move was perceived as a threat, not only to Roman commerce and trade but also to Rome's Gallic allies in Provence. Caesar realized that by mustering his foes and conquering the Helvetians, he could secure what he called *provincia nostre,* our province, and perhaps expand Rome's territories. The politician in him calculated the enormous gains any such victory would have on his prestige back in Rome.

So for the next ten years, from 59 to 49 BC, Julius Caesar commanded his Roman legions in Gaul in a series of battles against the Helvetii and Arvernii and various Germanic tribes until he found himself in control of the whole of Gaul. He described these campaigns in his *Commentaries,* surely one of the earliest accounts of military strategy as well as a great source of information about the Gallic and Teutonic peoples. Caesar earned for himself the reputation of not just a great historian but also one of the world's great generals. Interesting to think that Julius Caesar was a politician first who later became a military leader, as opposed to the more common sequence of successful generals entering politics. (Consider Napoleon, George Washington, Ulysses S. Grant, Eisenhower). But Caesar was an extraordinary man with a genius for leadership, whether civilian or military. After the Gallic wars, his enemies in the Senate feared his power and popularity, and consequently conspired with Pompey to force Caesar back into private life. So the Senate passed a law ordering Caesar to give up his command and return to Rome, which he interpreted correctly as tantamount to his ruination.

Julius Caesar did return to Rome in 48 BC, but at the head of his army. The famous episode of Caesar crossing the Rubicon, the small river that formed the northern boundary of Rome at that time, with the statement *Alea jacta est*, the die is cast, in defiance of the Roman Senate was a declaration of civil war. Rome was split between supporters of Julius Caesar and supporters of Pompey and the Senate. Caesar applied his leadership skills for speed, surprise, strategy, and logistics and forced Pompey's army to evacuate Italy, leaving Caesar in control.

Meanwhile, the cities in Gallia Provincia—Arles, Marseilles, Nîmes, and Narbonne—were forced to choose sides in the civil war, perhaps without realizing to what extent their future prosperity hinged on backing the winner. In the end, Marseilles supported Pompey over Caesar and dearly paid the price after Pompey's defeat and death when Caesar became master and dictator in 46 BC. Marseille lost favor as the primary center for trade and commerce, which was transferred to Nîmes and Arles with showers of Roman largesse.

During his dictatorship, Caesar enacted numerous reforms for the Roman state, including a reorganized legal system and equitable land distribution. He also introduced an improved calendar, which lasted for about 1,200 years before the Gregorian calendar was adopted. Some computer systems today still use Julian dates.

By the way, why did Caesar refuse to be crowned king? He had a very good reason. The traditional date for Rome's foundation is 758 BC, and Rome's early centuries were dominated by Etruscan kings, the Tarquinians. On the positive side, the Latinii recognized the superior culture and civilization of the Etruscans and were content for them to hold onto the highest power in early Rome. The level of influence the Etruscans had on Rome was profound. For example, what we think of as the Roman symbol of power, the bundle of rods surrounding an axe and bound with a leather strap—in Latin *faeces*, the origin of the word "facist"—is really Etruscan. That symbolism has lasted through the ages. Take another look at the statue of Abraham Lincoln in the Lincoln Memorial in Washington, DC, and you'll see the *faeces* represented on the arms of Lincoln's chair. In fact, many US federal and state government buildings display that ubiquitous symbol of power and law.

On the negative side, the Etruscan kings fell prey to the disease of tyranny that results from unlimited power. After a few centuries, the monarchy of the Tarquinians degenerated into corruption and vice, and the people of Rome rose up and expelled the last of the hated rulers. They then set up a republic, from *res publica*, of the people. Even though almost five hundred years had elapsed between the founding of the republic in 509 BC and Caesar's dictatorship, the Romans with their long memory retained a fear and hatred for the concept of king. Caesar knew if he accepted that title, the people's hatred would turn on him.

The final chapter of Caesar's amazing career was brief and violent. Thanks to Shakespeare and Hollywood, the scene is well-known: Cassius and Brutus lead a conspiracy to murder Caesar on the Ides of March, 44 BC; Caesar with twenty-three stab wounds falls at the foot of Pompey's statue, probably poetic justice by the dramatists; and Rome is plunged into yet another civil war. The remarkable personality who survived and triumphed out of that political contest was none other than Caesar's adopted grand-nephew, Octavian, known to us as the first Emperor of Rome, Augustus Caesar.

The story of Augustus and his legacy in Provence would require a dissertation of its own and will take this traveller into the era of the Roman Empire. So I added to my list of excursions a trip to the city in Provence beloved of Augustus, Nîmes.

CHAPTER 6

Going Native

Saturday Market in Uzès — Grocery Shopping Tips — Wine Tasting — Châteauneuf du Pape

One rule I learned early on was if you cannot be flexible in your travels, you'll be in for a lot of grief. On the other hand, allowing for impromptu changes to what should be only tentative plans can result in a lot of unexpected fun.

For example, one Saturday morning I had planned to go for a long hike outside the village and try to find the site of the ancient *oppidum* that I had heard about. Instead, a friend called to tell me that the town of Uzès was hosting its weekly Saturday market and that it was something I shouldn't miss. So I closed up the windows in the house, grabbed a frozen water bottle and my large canvas tote bag, and jumped in the car, first consulting the roadmap to refresh my memory of how to get to Uzès.

What a lovely drive it was, once I got outside the industrial zone of Bagnols sur Cèze. The fields were golden with sunflowers, interspersed with waving wheat, and the ever-present olive groves and vineyards. Everything you have heard about the narrow European roads is true, and in the South of France, the typical road is wide enough for about one and a half American cars and is frequently hemmed in with rows of huge plane trees. The landscape is very picturesque, which you enjoy until you see a large delivery truck fast approaching and know you have to squeeze in between the truck and the trees. In this and all situations on the small national roads, you are expected to drive like a bat out of hell, or else the other motorists behind you will take shocking chances to pass you. Funny—the French drive like crazy on the small, two-lane roads, and yet motor along like little old ladies on the *autoroutes*.

Negotiating through the roundabouts is particularly tricky here, but I do admire how the French drivers manage them. The accepted practice when approaching a roundabout is to touch the brake ever so slightly, take a quick glance to the left to judge instantly the speed of the approaching cars, and then jam on the accelerator to jump in between the oncoming cars. If you miss your turn-off route—one of the spokes radiating from the traffic circle—no need to panic; just continue careening around almost on two wheels until you find your way back. I've been known to make two circuits because I missed my turnoff the first time, not that I recommend you make a habit of driving around and around the roundabouts.

❧ ❧

The Provençal markets are an old and prized tradition, and a town's right to hold a market was a source of pride, as well as enormous profits, and was fiercely defended for centuries. The practice of granting of a town's market license goes back to medieval times. The town of Uzès was the seat of the bishopric, and the Bishop of Uzès, who in 1223 obtained the license for the market, controlled many villages in the area, including our village. So the *samedi marche*, Saturday market, was very important to the region. Other towns had market days on other days of the week and kept those days for many centuries, too; for example, in Barjac and Goudargues, the market day was Wednesday, and in Vaison-la-Romaine market day was Tuesday.

I was not the only one headed to the market in Uzès. As soon as I exited the last roundabout into town, I had to come to a screeching stop and saw a line of cars in front of me and a line of cars forming behind me. Where did they all come from? *Sacre bleu!* And I had just passed a sign that said *parking gratuite*, free parking. Realizing my mistake, I did a quick U-turn and headed back to the parking lot, hoping for an empty spot. I had to park on what was a sidewalk, grateful that my compact car could squeeze in that tight spot. Then I trudged up the hill, following the signs to the *Centre Ville*, the town center. I soon found myself in a parade of pedestrians with shopping bags streaming along the street toward central Uzès, while the line of cars inched along beside us with their scowling occupants. When I arrived, the entire town center, which on other days seemed a bit sleepy, buzzed with activity. The area had been converted to an outdoor shopping zone made up of a long string of tables and carts in the streets and filling the plazas, some covered with canopies for protection from the sun, but most set in the shade of the large plane trees.

What an amazing variety of goods, and all regional! There were vendors selling jewelry, soaps, olive oil, wine, household goods and kitchen utensils, colorful Provençal pottery and tiles, wicker baskets, beautiful quilts and linens, tablecloths and rolls of Provençal fabrics, and clothing and shoes for adults and children. There were all sorts of food vendors selling bread and pastries, vegetables and fruits, orange juice, ice cream, and sandwiches. One huge table was devoted to herbs, with dozens of small, cloth-lined wicker baskets filled with herbs and spices, all neatly labeled. There were several butcher carts with the specialties of the region, cured hams, sausages, and a variety of pâtés. All the restaurants on the street were open, and the outdoor tables were full. The town was packed to capacity, and all I could do was go with the flow.

I wandered by the classic mimes dressed as Harlequin or Golden Aphrodite on their street-corner pedestals and listened to the buskers playing guitar and accordion and singing French café songs. A Dixieland jazz trio was entertaining the crowds; they would have looked and sounded at home in New Orleans. The air was thick with music and the aroma of roasted chicken and olives and herbs. I was on the lookout for some tablecloths and lavender soap, and checked the selections to find the lowest prices. Even with my halting French, I didn't have much trouble talking to the vendors, and almost everyone was patient and friendly. One young lady selling souvenir towels had lived in San Francisco and spoke English very well, and I had a nice chat with her. I lingered at a table piled with used books and selected an old pamphlet entitled *Les Origines de Nîmes*. I had to hold myself back from other purchases, remembering that whatever I bought I would have to carry through three airports or leave behind at the house, unseen until next year.

The shadows had lengthened, my frozen water bottle had long since melted in the heat, and my feet were tired, so I decided to end my shopping spree with my treasures and head home. Just before leaving, I stopped to buy a small ceramic cicada, called *cigale*, the ubiquitous motif of Provence. Many of the tablecloths, towels, napkins, and pottery for sale at the market are emblazoned with this noisy insect. Their chirping is constant this time of the summer, and I've been told they are a sign of good luck. I planned to keep this last purchase for myself; it would tuck away nicely in my backpack.

∽ ⌒

In general, grocery shopping in French cities or, indeed, European cities or—okay, let's be honest—anywhere outside the United States involves some adjustment. Americans are accustomed to having our stores open twenty-four hours a day, seven days a week, and our groceries bagged for us in free bags—paper or plastic?—by efficient, cheerful supermarket staff. *Au contraire, mon vieux!* Here are a few items to consider when going native at the French *supermarche*:

1. The shopping carts, called *les chariots*—not at all like ancient Egyptian chariots—are chained together under a covered kiosk in the parking lot. To release a cart, you need a one euro coin or token, which stays in the chain lock on your cart. When you replace the cart, you can retrieve your coin by re-chaining the cart. Once I obtained a shopping cart token, I kept it in my pocket for future grocery trips.

2. You need to bag your own groceries and pay for your shopping bags, which I think is a sound practice for the environment. The going rate at the *CarreFour* was 0.50 euro for a small bag and 0.75 euro for a large bag, which adds up quickly. You will train yourself to take used bags with you for subsequent trips.

3. When you select your vegetables or fruits, you must weigh them at the produce section. There are usually an insufficient number of scales nearby, but they are easy to spot because of the queue that has formed behind the little old lady weighing her veggies. The scale prints out a sticker that you place on the plastic bag. Do not expect the young women at the checkout counters to do this for you; they

will send you back to the produce section with a scornful look.

4.   At the checkout line, you unload your cart, using the separators to keep your items away from the fellow's in front of you. The checker, usually a young woman, who is always seated at the cash register which restricts her reach and which she makes no effort to extend, scans your purchases once they are directly in front of her on the conveyer belt. You should always greet her with a friendly *bonjour*. You will need to watch as your items are rung up, while selecting a credit card that will work—they don't always—and then bag your items yourself and get the bags into your cart without getting too flustered because of the line forming behind you.

5.   Probably the most difficult item for an American to remember is the store's opening and closing hours. Do not assume the supermarkets will be open twenty-four hours a day, seven days a week; that convenience does not exist in the South of France or, for that matter, almost anywhere in Europe. The closing hours in summer are different than in winter, with closing at 8:00 pm in the summer and earlier in winter. The smaller shops may also be closed about two hours in the early afternoon and reopen for the evening. Don't believe the posted hours for the small shops; it is best to ask. I seemed always to get it wrong and would start my power-shopping just before closing hours and would be put back out on the curb, frustrated. Your routines are dictated by shop hours. You also need to be aware of bank holidays; everything will be closed, and you may have to subsist on yesterday's stale baguette for breakfast.

6. Last and very important, don't bother being in a hurry. It doesn't do you any good.

At the grocery store, I would usually take a few moments to observe the variety of humanity around me in the checkout line, from the young mothers and their squirming kids, to the huge teenage boys buying beer and snacks to scarf down while watching soccer games on TV, to the elderly couple looking for the best values, to the flirty, middle-aged men chatting up the cashier girls. Not much different than at home.

I was most interested in observing the locals' clothing styles. I wanted to blend in, and I certainly didn't want my clothes to give me away as a foreigner. Many years ago when my daughter and I travelled through Ireland, we would step into a pub, and before we even opened our mouths, the man at the bar would ask, "So what part of America are you ladies from?" as if we had neon signs above our heads saying "American Tourist." In an effort not to make the same mistakes, I avoided white sneakers, T-shirts with English phrases, and anything with an American flag. But glancing around I couldn't detect much difference in the way the people dressed here compared to back in Colorado. It seemed that khaki shorts, tank tops, sandals, and sunglasses were the standard summertime vacation-holiday attire here as well as at home. Perhaps when I spend the winter, I might notice a difference, in which case I planned on buying clothes here to wear for the winter months.

∽ ∾

One of the greatest pleasures of travelling in *le Midi*, the South of France, was the chance to sample the regional wines under the appellation of *Côtes du Rhône*; in fact, it is an essential activity. One should not visit this region without taking the time to discover the local vineyards.

Wine tasting is a wonderfully enjoyable activity anywhere in France; in Languedoc, the region of ancient Provence on the west side of the Rhône River, it is a special pleasure because it will take you to many of the most renowned vineyards in France, which happen also to be in some amazingly picturesque villages. This region is home to *Châteauneuf du Pape*, a particularly famous and fine wine of its own *Appellation d'Origine Contrôllée* (AOC) that I had heard about from my knowledgeable friends. But it is truly astonishing how many other *Domaine* names and vineyards there are in Languedoc, of which you get only a glimpse while driving around. In fact, Languedoc probably has the most vineyards per capita of any region in France. Though our village is on the northeast edge of Languedoc in the *Département* of Gard, it too is surrounded with vineyards. I was amused to realize the walking distance from the village to buy wine at *Domaine Bel Air* is less than to buy bread in St. Michel.

My favorite neighboring *Domaines* for buying wine were Tavel and Lirac, both very pretty villages. The proprietors in the wine shops were friendly, and the wine cellars were nicely stocked with my favorite rosés, as well as other Provençal produce. I particularly liked to buy the wine glasses with the domain name and logo delicately engraved on them, and I acquired a smart collection.

Most of the best vineyard châteaux are open much of the day for *degustation*, wine tasting. It is free, but don't go just for the free samples. Go with the intention of buying, if you like what you taste. I could never leave a wine tasting without buying at least half a dozen bottles; I always found something I liked, and I thought it would be rude if I didn't buy after a *degustation* because I had taken up the proprietor's time and sampled their stock.

Of course I had no idea how to buy wine until Kate and Marc introduced me to the tradition when we travelled together in the Loire Valley some years ago. At that time they bought several cases of French wine to take back to Berlin, which put such a load on the rear suspension of the BMW that I was worried. At least whenever we were staying in the village and went on local wine-tasting excursions, we could bring the cases back to the house for storage in their wine cellar.

On a particularly memorable outing a few summers ago, Marc, Kate, and I ended up at a Châteauneuf du Pape winery called *le Château de Vaudieu*. We had passed it several times before, but every time we stopped, it was past tasting hours. To make sure we didn't make that mistake again, we arrived at eleven o'clock in the morning. You might think that wine tasting just a few hours after breakfast is not such a great idea. Well, if the thought bothers you, just remember that you are really only anticipating lunch by a handful of minutes. And if you do manage to hit the *Château de Vaudieu* in particular for wine tasting, you will not be disappointed because both the reds and the whites can be quite striking.

For wine-tasting we drove east across the Rhône, past Orange, and merged on the country road south to get to the town of Châteauneuf, meaning new castle. The town dates from the fourteenth century when the papacy moved from Rome to Avignon. Though now in ruins, the château on the hill above the town was one of many fine mansions built when the power and wealth of the papacy took up residence in the South of France. In fact, the popes caused these vineyards to be planted and the viticulture established to supply their tables with what they missed from their life in Rome. For this reason the wine bottles of Châteauneuf du Pape have the papal insignia, the tiara and the crossed keys.

Wine shop in Châteauneuf du Pape

To reach the *Domaine Vaudieu*, we passed through the narrow streets of Châteauneuf and headed out into the countryside on narrow roads. We shared the road with a few tractors, tall and narrow for working between the rows of grapevines. The turnoff to reach Vaudieu's château took us down an enchanting drive, flanked by picturesque cypress trees and the vineyards themselves. In the midst of the fields of shining grape leaves was a small medieval tower, and in the distance I could see the hill town of Châteauneuf, which we had just passed through, with the castle ruins clearly silhouetted on the crest of the hill. We came upon the great stone and iron gates of Vaudieu, behind which is the eighteenth-century château that serves as the business offices and the owners' residence. If the entry gates are open, which they were, they are ready for business.

We parked just inside the main courtyard spread with white limestone gravel and noted the signs to the main tasting room through a portal flanked with columns and wine barrels with flowers. The château cat, a sweet little orange tabby, was our welcoming committee, though soon one of the proprietors emerged from the château walking across the gravel courtyard in the sunshine and escorted us into the tasting room. Wine tasting can be an art for experts; for the rest of us, it is a process of learning what you like and how to tell with a sniff or sip. You don't even have to swallow all the different samples in order to get an idea whether you want to make a purchase. In fact, with as many as four whites and four reds to try, you may not want to swallow even the tiniest tastes, especially if you are the one driving. I was thankful that day I was not driving!

When we went there, the years on offer were particularly fine. The *Domaine* normally provides the potential buyer with a selection in age and in care taken with the particular vintages. Sometimes it is a question of taste, so to speak, and sometimes it is a question of quality. But you'll never know which until you try. For us, the

2006 and 2008 vintages were quite fine, each with their own characteristics. The proprietors, who explain their wines as you sample them, are invariably helpful, even when they have a limited command of English. A wine tasting is actually a good time to test your French language skills because the proprietors will be quite friendly and forgiving—and grateful—for your efforts. In my case, when travelling with Marc and Kate, I was never bold enough to attempt French, and I let them do all the talking. We left there quite satisfied, lumbering back with four cases of wine—a promise of pleasant evenings to come!

Though the Châteauneuf du Pape from the Domaine Château de Vaudieu is indeed a wine you may be able to find in classy shops, don't just stick with the names you recognize. By visiting random wineries, you may not discover a new great vintage, but you will certainly be richer for the experience.

∽ ∾

Remembering the interesting-looking castle ruin above the town of Châteauneuf, I decided to return by myself later so I could get a closer look. The town itself had a country village feel to it with buildings and churches dating from the late Middle Ages, shops and restaurants with local patrons, and open squares decorated with flowers and benches for tired pedestrians. I parked in front of the municipal gymnasium and swimming pool, and set off to find the château ruins on the hill. After following the signs and asking for directions, I came to what seemed to be the edge of town and had no idea where to turn. I spotted a small arena with about three rows of benches tucked into the bottom of a hill, its purpose a mystery. Too small for soccer, too large for *boules*, I thought maybe it was a rural bullring for local *ferias*?

I continued on what seemed to be an alleyway and found the street that led up to the château. The street was lined with fine homes with gardens. One of the houses had been turned into a restaurant, and my growling stomach reminded me that I had skipped lunch. At last I climbed up what seemed to be a thousand steps to the château, which was really only a shell of what had probably been the great hall. The carved stones lining the entrance doorway had been stripped away, leaving only the corbel-arch stonework of the walls, which showed how the Gothic arch had been originally formed. The walls were so thick that the glassless arched windows had stone benches on each side as wide as the walls were thick— very medieval looking, except for the metal screens to keep tourists from falling out. The wind at that height was powerful and whistled through the windows and inside the bare walls. Looking over the edge of the parapet, I got a dizzying view of the town below and the Rhône River in the distance.

I wandered along the road behind the château ruin where I found a small vineyard and wondered whether these grapes were a Châteauneuf designation. Smooth, round stones, about the size of a man's fist, were piled at the base of each vine, carefully and deliberately placed. I remembered when we visited the *Domaine Mordorée* that the vintner had explained how the growers put the stones at the vine roots to absorb the sun's heat during the day and emit heat at night to warm the roots. The attention given to the smallest detail by the experienced and skilled vintners was quite impressive.

Walking back through the town, I passed so many wine shops that I lost count. Each had hand-lettered signs with the daily specials; some shops offered snacks with the wine tasting. Eye-pleasing barrels of flowers were set under pointed arch Gothic tracery windows, and small tables and chairs were set out to entice the tourists to stop. Even the air seemed to hold a faint aroma of wine, perfume of the local industry. Some of the wine shops were decorated with the emblem of the Châteauneuf du Pape in a juxtaposition of modern marketing and ancient stone buildings. I resolved to do my utmost to keep the wine business humming, supporting the tradition and history of the *Côte du Rhône* appellation. I promised myself that when I returned home to Colorado and went shopping for wine, I would make a habit of asking for Tavel or Lirac rosés of the Rhône Valley. It is a treat to enjoy wines from the region that I am by now quite familiar. If I am feeling flush, for it is rather expensive, I will pick up a bottle of a Châteauneuf du Pape, when I can find it, remembering the sights and aromas of this charming village.

CHAPTER 7

More Romans

Exploring Nîmes and Pont du Gard — Augustus and Agrippa — Visit to Les Baux de Provence and Glanum

We struggle to define civilization, but, like obscenity, we know it when we see it. At the end of excursion days, after exhausting myself searching for ancient sites or studying artifacts in museums, I would go back to the village and spend my evenings at the house below the château, sitting in the upper living room, gazing through the windows as the sun set over the valley, and watching the clouds traverse the sky from the west to east while the sky turned from a warm golden glow to a deep dark blue. I usually had music softly playing; how soothing the Bach Goldberg Variations were to a tired traveller. Feeling quite civilized, often with a glass of wine, I read my history books. Of course, I had nothing to do with the restoration of this wonderful stone house or the making of the wine or the recording of this brilliant music or the rediscovery of antiquities, but I felt that I could include myself with those artists and builders and vintners and composers because I knew and appreciated civilization when I was immersed in it. And in southern France I was surrounded by the products of two thousand years of civilization. *Now hold on*, I told myself. Today my contribution to civilization consisted of doing two loads of laundry and setting the digital clock on the stove so it stopped flashing 00:00. Let's not get too carried away.

The evenings served another purpose: to plan the next day's outing. Ah, just the thing! I decided it was time to visit Nîmes, the city of Augustus and the site of some of the most spectacular Roman buildings in the South of France, indisputable evidence of civilization.

The story of Roman Gaul cannot be complete without Augustus, the first emperor of Rome, who gave his name to an age. It is difficult to overstate the impact Augustus had on the course of Western civilization. He was born into the family of the Octavii in 63 BC and was the grandnephew on his mother's side of Gaius Julius Caesar. However, his father's family was of the lower equestrian order, whereas the Julii were of the senatorial patrician class. Nevertheless, Octavian was well educated and earned the favorable notice of his uncle, who eventually adopted him. When Caesar was assassinated in 44 BC, Octavian was studying in Illyria, modern Turkey, and at the news he returned to Rome and learned that Caesar had named him as his principle heir. Octavian took the name Caesar to honor his uncle and forced the Senate to make him a Tribune and hunt down Caesar's assassins. At the age of nineteen, he named himself consul, formed his personal army, and demanded the Senate to rubber-stamp the appointment. In 43 BC Octavian, along with Mark Anthony and Marcus Lepidus, served on the Triumvirate commissioned by the Senate to reorganize the government. After sending Lepidus into exile in 36 BC, Octavian governed in the west and Anthony in the east until 31 BC, and then by himself as sole ruler for another forty-five years. The Senate and

Commons voted him lifelong tribunician power. He did not want the title of censor, although he did hold a public census three times, one of which was cited in the New Testament Gospel of St. Luke. Octavian assumed the office of chief priest, called *pontifex maximus*, and used that office to restore the veneration of the ancient religious practices. He promoted many civic causes, improved public buildings—late in life he famously boasted, "I found Rome a city of brick and left it a city of marble"—built roads and aqueducts, and established an armed police to combat bandits. His hand was evident in virtually every aspect of Roman social and legal systems.

Octavian had with him during his rise to power his boyhood friend Marcus Vipsanius Agrippa, with whose help he defeated the forces of Mark Anthony and Cleopatra at the Battle of Actium in 31 BC. The victory gave Octavian sole power in Rome. The suicide of Cleopatra, who was the last of the Ptolomies, ended the Greek dynasty in Egypt that dated from the end of Alexander the Great's empire, and Octavian turned the Kingdom of Egypt into a Roman province.

Octavian was granted the title *Augustus* by the Senate in 27 BC. Some in the Senate had wished him to be called Romulus after the mythical founder of Rome, but they settled on Augustus, *august*, meaning increase in dignity. Augustus was careful, as his great-uncle Julius had been, to avoid the title *king*, although he was king in everything but name. To be sure, the Senate seemed anxious to vote him whatever title he would accept short of king. Instead, Augustus called his rule the principate, from *princeps*, the first man of the state, which represented a compromise between a monarchy and a republic. His title *pontifex maximus* referred to the head of the principal college of priests in the ancient Roman religion. That title survives today to refer to the pope in Rome, the pontiff. And pontifex comes from a Latin word *pontis* or *pons*, meaning bridge. So the implication was that the pontifex served as the bridge-maker between heaven and earth. Every time I drive over the *Pont Charles Martel*, I think of the etymology of the French word *pont*.

The façade of a republican government, carefully constructed by Augustus, lasted until the reign of Domitian (81–96 AD) when it was acknowledged as an empire and an autocracy. But the empire as built by Augustus survived in the West until 476 AD and continued in the East as the Byzantine Empire until the fall of Constantinople in 1453 AD. When Augustus died in 14 AD at the age of seventy-six, the period of Roman history he oversaw came to be called *Pax Romana*, a time of relative peace and stability that enabled the advance of Western civilization. Quite an achievement for a remarkable man from obscure plebian-equestrian origins.

But as much as we know of the life of Augustus, little is recorded of the silent hero of Augustus's success, Marcus Vipsanius Agrippa. He also was born around 63 BC and was educated with Octavian, in spite of the fact that his father was an unimportant provincial. When Julius Caesar was assassinated, Agrippa, who was in Illyria with Octavian, returned to Rome with him and remained his faithful supporter and his best military general for the rest of his life. In fact, Agrippa became Augustus's son-in-law when he married Augustus's only daughter, Julia, in 21 BC. That marriage produced five children, two of whom, Lucius and Gaius, Augustus adopted as his heirs. In addition to his military leadership, Agrippa also served as Roman consul and from 37 BC as *aedile*, an official in charge of public buildings and civic improvements. As such, he undertook numerous building projects and repairs in Rome, including constructing more aqueducts and cleaning out the *cloaca maxima*, the main sewer in Rome.

In 40 BC the Treaty of Brundisium had given Octavian control of the West, and to counter Marc Antony's power in the eastern provinces, he sent Agrippa to Provincia Gallia Narbonensis to act as governor. Agrippa spent two years, from 39 to 37 BC, in Gaul, and during that time he initiated and oversaw the construction of many public buildings, roads, and aqueducts, the remains of which astonish us even today. The sophisticated engineering skills of the Roman builders, hydrologists, and architects are a wonder to behold, and the

Chained crocodile, the emblem of Nîmes

cities of Provence, such as Nîmes, Arles, and Orange, are justly proud
of their heritage. Nîmes in particular was favored by Augustus. As a
result of Augustus's fondness, Nîmes received magnificent municipal buildings, an arena, a circus, and temples. The lush agricultural
lands surrounding the city were parceled out to the veterans of his
Egyptian legions for their retirement as gentlemen farmers. Today
the emblem of the city of Nîmes shows a Nile crocodile chained to
a palm tree to memorialize Augustus's largesse to his Roman soldiers
for their faithful service in Egypt. Augustus may have visited the city
himself when, according to Cassius Dio, the Roman historian of the
second century AD, he journeyed to Gaul in 27 BC and again from
16 to 15 BC when it was called Colonia Augusta Nemausensis, after
Nemausa, a local deity of a sacred spring.

೧೦ ೧೦

How fortunate for me to be staying in a village only forty minutes from Nîmes; it was possible to visit every day if I wished.
Driving southbound on the small national road approaching
Nîmes, I noticed the colorful flags bearing the emblem of Nîmes,
the crocodile chained to a palm tree, waving from tall poles lining
the road. The city is now very large and sprawling with the modern
sections on the outskirts. I followed the jumble of road signs to the
Centre Ville and pulled into the underground parking facility nearest
the Jardins de la Fontaine, the Fountain Gardens. From here on I would
be walking and was already anticipating how footsore I would be
by the end of the day. Just looking at the map of all the Roman
artifacts, I could see why this city is called "the Rome of France,"
and I knew the sites were not all within easy walking distance.

In nineteenth-century history books, the city of Nîmes is
spelled Nismes. When studying French, I learned that for a vowel
written with a circumflex (as in â, ê, î, ô, û), the circumflex may

be a substitute for a letter that was eliminated from the old, obsolete form of the word. So Nismes of the old-school textbooks has become Nîmes. The original name, Nemauses, dates from before the Romans came to Gaul, and we can only guess at how the name changed over time.

The old sections of the city look vaguely familiar—French urban construction, made up of eighteenth- and nineteenth-century stone apartment buildings, four or five stories high, shuttered windows with balconies, terra-cotta tiled roofs, street-level shops lining shady boulevards. I set out for the first site, the *Maison Carrée*. Even though I knew what this Roman temple looked like from photographs, I was still surprised to come upon this amazing structure after walking down what seemed to be an ordinary street. This building may be one of the most famous in all France and is certainly the best-preserved Roman temple outside of Italy. It is said Napoleon Bonaparte was so inspired by the elegant simplicity and symmetry of this temple that it was the model for the design of the church *La Madeleine* in Paris. It was a bit difficult to imagine how the temple had looked in its original setting, now that it stands in the middle of an eighteenth-century open plaza. The level of the plaza is about 1.5 meters above the level of the ancient street, a forum that had been lined with columns. Beneath the modern sidewalk, one can see the remnants of some of the columns that once had graced the original forum two thousand years ago. The *Maison Carrée* dates from the first century BC, built in honor of Augustus's two grandsons, Gaius and Lucius, the sons of Agrippa, and its construction has been attributed to Agrippa. It was saved from destruction when it was converted to a Christian church and later served as a city hall. Inside is a small museum with original sculptures uncovered from sites around Roman Nîmes. The building is in an amazing state of preservation and is still functional; the generous steps of the podium are used today by the young people as a meeting and socializing locale.

Maison Carrée with Carré d'Art in distance

Wandering southwest and following the signs, I came upon the arena, probably one of the finest Roman amphitheatres in existence. I cannot begin to describe how huge it is; I could hardly take it all in as I walked around the perimeter, straining my neck looking up. Built in the first century BC, it could hold 24,000 spectators, eager for bread and circuses, on thirty-four levels of steps. The entrance galleries were designed for easy access and egress, which permitted the entire arena to be evacuated within about five minutes. How many modern arenas could boast that? Again, this architectural marvel survived the centuries by remaining useful for succeeding generations. The Visigoths turned it into a fortress, and the poor of the Middle Ages were permitted to build small houses and chapels within the arena for protection. In the mid-1800s the arena was restored to its original function and today is used for concerts, plays, and the *ferias*, the bullfights.

I found my way back to the *Jardins de la Fontaine*, the Fountain Gardens, and the site of the original spring of Nemausus. This formal garden architecture looked decidedly seventeenth century Baroque, perhaps of the same vintage as Versailles, with marble vases and statues of nymphs and cupids and carved garlands on the balustrade surrounding the pools. This pleasant, grassy park in the middle of the old city featured gravel walks and open areas where groups of old men played *boules*.

By this time my feet were aching, and I was quite ready to continue my discoveries of Roman Nîmes by car. Emerging from the parking garage, I drove to the *castellum divisorium*, the point of arrival of the Nîmes aqueduct, of which the famous *Pont du Gard* is but one section. The *castellum divisorium*, a large, circular water distribution tank, was built into the side of a hill on the northern edge of the city; it was rediscovered in 1844 and is recognized as a rare surviving example of ancient hydrology. The Nîmes aqueduct fed water from a spring near Uzès along a route fifty kilometers long to enter the city at this distribution point. A lock system was used to distribute the water in the large circular basin in five different directions, through clay pipes and out to the whole city. It is estimated that this basin supplied twenty thousand cubic meters of water per day, which is about four hundred liters for each of the fifty thousand inhabitants of Nemausus. The Romans were simply amazing engineers.

I decided to forgo visiting other sites in the city and instead drove out to the *Pont du Gard*, which was a short fifteen minutes away. This aqueduct is an UNESCO World Heritage Site, to which the extensive car park with spaces for many tour buses attests. Because the day was getting on, I decided to bypass the museum, which looked excellent, and headed straight for the *Pont*. Again, I was stunned at the immense size; photos are inadequate in conveying the size of this monumental structure. Agrippa is traditionally cited as responsible for the construction of this aqueduct, but whether it was built in 19 BC under his distant patronage or between 39 and 37 BC when he was actively building in Gaul is not clear. In any event, the course of the aqueduct that brought water from Uzès to Nîmes required a bridge to span the deep valley cut by the Gardon River, and what an engineering feat this is! The bridge is made up of three runs of arches on three levels built of enormous blocks of stone from a nearby quarry, some weighing an estimated six tons; that were shaped and fitted together without mortar. These giant stone arches appear in the middle of a wilderness, which gives the bridge all the more startling effect. The lowest run is made up of six huge arches, the middle run has eleven arches, and the topmost run is made up of thirty-five small arches covering a length of 275 meters. This top run of arches contained the closed channel for carrying the water. The total height of the bridge above the river at low level is about fifty meters, comparable to a fifteen-story building. The first level includes a pedestrian walkway, which had been used as a toll-bridge for wagons and cattle. Even with its utilitarian function, the bridge fell into disrepair over the centuries

Pont du Gard

until the Emperor Napoleon III, who idolized everything Roman, ordered the restoration in 1855, preserving it for posterity.

Perhaps because I live in the western United States where water is scarce and precious, I think hydraulic engineering is fascinating. The Roman solution to the problem of supplying water to Nîmes, a city of fifty thousand thirsty Gallo-Romans, was the construction of this aqueduct. Even though the spring at Uzès is only twenty kilometers away from Nîmes as the crow flies, the aqueduct channel covered a meandering distance of fifty kilometers to ensure the slope of the channel was not too steep or too shallow for the controlled flow of water. The altitude of Uzès is only about seventeen meters above Nîmes, and if my math is correct, the channel has approximately a 0.034 percent gradient. About thirty-five kilometers of the aqueduct is underground, some of it tunneling through rock, and the other fifteen kilometers of the aqueduct is exposed above ground, in closed channels carried on gently sloping walls, or on bridges such as this. What a marvel of organization and engineering. And consider: the Romans built aqueducts all over the Empire, from North Africa to Turkey to England; the longest yet discovered covers nearly one hundred kilometers.

Among the hordes of visitors, I climbed to the top of the bridge to get a look at the water channel, now unused, to see what was left of the tiles and stone covers that protected the water from dirt, debris, and evaporation. It was a beautiful, warm day, and the river below was full of cavorting sunbathers and young men diving off the limestone bluffs into the river. I thought this scene must be similar to those played out in years past, such as when the French king Charles IX visited with his royal retinue in 1564 to picnic on the banks of the Gardon River flowing beneath the *Pont du Gard*.

Walking back over the bridge, I spotted a sign reading *Mémoires de Garrigue*, "Stories of a Mediterranean Landscape," pointing to what looked like the entrance to a garden that seemed to be ignored by everyone else. After checking the time, I thought I'd give it a look and set off to discover a large parkland that has been set aside as a natural habitat, preserving the preindustrial, agricultural appearance of this region. The path took me past bucolic farmlands—examples of a long agricultural history. The fields had been planted with the variety of crops, as they had been as early as five hundred years ago, demonstrating techniques as well as experimentation. Olive trees were planted within the rows of grapevines to allow the vines to climb the trees for support. Fields of grains, perhaps wheat and barley, displayed crops of many colors interspersed with vegetables. I walked by one field that contained a stand of ancient mulberry trees neatly spaced in regular rows. A sign informed me that these trees had been planted by the order of the French King Henry IV in 1595 to provide food for the silkworms to support the silk industry that had been introduced into this region in the 1400s. Wandering through the habitat, I found a dry-stone *borie* from the 1800s and another small, crumbling section of the Nîmes aqueduct, this one unnoticed and overlooked in the shadow of the stupendous *Pont du Gard*. After a pleasant stroll away from the throngs of tourists, I headed back to the car park to find the car and drive home, regretting that I had run out of time and determined to return to visit the museum.

∾ ℃

After a few days, I again felt the need to explore more Roman sites, and I decided on a daytrip to Glanum, the amazing ancient town just south of St-Remy-de-Provence. I mapped out various routes, trying to avoid the tolls on the *autoroute*, and set the alarm for very early the next morning because I had a drive of about seventy kilometers ahead of me.

Up at dawn, I had a quick cup of tea, packed a lunch, and headed south. I had to contend with a lot of what passes here for rush-hour traffic—delivery trucks, housewives, workers, and salesmen, all trying to squeeze through the same roundabouts as I was. It occurred to me—here we were, scrambling to get to our destinations along roads that probably were first laid out by the Romans in the first century. Funny to think that I and my fellow commuters may have been travelling on the route the Carthaginian general Hannibal and his army and elephants used for the invasion of Italy in 218 BC. But instead of a quest for military glory, some of us were on a quest to get to the *boulangerie* before it sold out of baguettes.

The route wound around from the south to the east along what had been the ancient *Via Domitia* that linked Italy with Hispania through Gallia Narbonensis. This route was truly legendary; the mythical hero Hercules was supposed to have travelled along this way to Spain on one of his Labors. The Roman road was constructed in 117 BC by the proconsul Gnaeus Domitius Ahenobarbus, an ancestor of the emperor Nero. Crossing the coastal plain from the Pyrenees to the Alps, the *Via Domitia* would lead to the antiquities of Glanum.

What a beautiful summer morning—bright blue sky with puffy cumulus clouds and the early green of the vineyards and olive orchards. I was becoming quite comfortable on this route because I had travelled it to reach Nîmes and Laudun. However, when I made the interchange from the N86 to the D99 eastbound at Remoulin, I was in, for me, uncharted territory. The Rhône River loomed large on the road ahead, and I got a glimpse of the famous twelfth-century castle of Good King René as I sped across the bridge at Tarascon, vowing to return another day. I followed the signs to St-Remy-de-Provence and soon found myself driving up a steep, winding road into a landscape of pale limestone outcroppings. This was the western edge of the *Chaine des Alpilles*, the mountain chain of rugged limestone formations amid scrubland of holm and downy oak and gorse, called *garrigue*, from a Provençal word, *garriga*, meaning oak. The scenery reminded me of the Garden of the Gods in Colorado, except the color of the rocks of the Alpilles was white instead of red. Straining my eyes to read the French road signs, I caught sight of a sign pointing to Les Beaux, a place I had wanted to see but was not on today's itinerary. Making a snap decision to alter my plan, I turned toward Les Beaux and found myself in a tight, winding canyon of dusty pale rocks, barely able to keep my eyes on the road because the landscape was so curiously spooky. Nearing the top, I got my first look at the fortress ruins of Les Beaux, the medieval home of one of the most powerful and independent lords of Provence.

There was no place to park in the medieval town; all the car parks were full, so I left the car along the road and hiked to the top. The entrance to the lower town has a visitor-friendly center and a large sign with details of the history of Les Baux. The sign described how the rocky heights of the fortress, 280 meters above the plains, have sheltered humans since the Bronze Age. In the tenth century, it was the center of the lords of Les Baux, who claimed descent from Balthazar, whom they called Bautezar, one of the Three Magi. For this reason the ancient coat of arms of Les Baux includes the star of Bethlehem and the motto in the Provençal language, *A l'asard Bautezar*, "To chance, Balthazar." The lords of Les Baux, within their impregnable rock fortress, were able to stay independent of the counts of Provence for hundreds of years. The feudal fame of Les Baux rested on the tradition of poetry and music from the troubadours who found protection here to create ballads of courtly love. This became a center of what we think of as the Age of Chivalry, when gallant knights errant sang the praises of the noble and elegant ladies, and the epic poetry of the Provencal troubadours, the *chansons de geste*, inspired Western literature and became part of our heritage.

Les Baux could not remain independent. When the last princess of Les Baux, Alix, died in 1426, it was taken over by the counts of Provence, and in 1486 Provence became part of France. In 1528 Les Baux came under the protection of Constable Anne de Montmorency and, for a brief time, was prosperous. However, Montmorency, as a Huguenot, exposed the inhabitants to the wrath of the Catholic monarchy during the Religious Wars. At last, in 1632 King Louis XIII ordered the destruction of the fortress and the village, and even demanded the inhabitants foot the bill. The discovery in 1822 of the mineral bauxite, the aluminum ore named for this town, provided some temporary economic improvements to the much-reduced population, but when the mines played out, what remained of Les Baux became what it is today, almost completely dependent on tourism.

There was a prodigious crop of tourists that day; I never made the guided tour of the castle ruins because of the daunting queue that had formed at the entrance, and I didn't want to waste time waiting in line. Instead I wandered around town, checking out the souvenir shops and getting some photos. At the top of the street, I found the Church of St. Vincent with its ancient square bell tower and went inside. The interior was well kept with flowers, candles, and fine carved stone Romanesque decorations. The right side of the interior was bare rock because the church had been built into the side of the hill. A sign above one of the side chapels acknowledged gratitude for the preservation of this church to the royal House of Grimaldi, the rulers of the Principality of Monaco. I later learned the current Prince of Monaco, Albert II, claims "Lord of Les Baux" in his string of titles, which of course the government of France does not recognize. Nevertheless, the prince seems to maintain his hereditary duty to Les Baux.

It was time to continue on to my original destination, Glanum. Heading north on a road that seemed to be a small pass through the Alpille hills, I found the car park for *Les Antiques de Glanum* and was lucky enough to get a spot under some trees. Seeing photographs of *Les Antiques*, two Roman monuments from the first century BC, did not sufficiently prepare me; I was awed by their beauty, size, and state of preservation.

The taller monument, which is eighteen meters high and called the mausoleum, but really a cenotaph marking what was probably the Glanum necropolis, is built in three sections. The square base of the pediment is decorated with a carved frieze depicting battles and hunting scenes, the midsection is an arch with four bays looking triumphant, and the top is a round *tholos* of Corinthian columns containing the statues of two young men, perhaps Lucius and Marcus who, according to the carved inscription, dedicated the monument to their parents, members of the *gens Julii*, the same family as Julius Caesar. Only the sculpted pine cone that should surmount the conical roof is missing. The monument is in a truly amazing state for being more than two thousand years old.

The arch is not as well preserved. It straddles what was the road into Glanum and has only one passage opening, unlike the arch in Orange, which has three. The upper third of the arch is missing, and the exposed stone and rubble core was covered with tiles to preserve what was left from eroding away. The interior ceiling of the arch is coffered in hexagonal panels, which reminded me of the interior of the dome of the Pantheon in Rome. The exterior was decorated with columns and symbolic sculptures, badly eroded but still remarkable.

Continuing south, I walked past a small limestone quarry that dated from the Christian era, but may have also supplied stone for the city. The entrance to Glanum was through a visitor hall that introduced the story of the excavations, featured copies of the sculptures and paintings, showed scale models of the city in the Hellenic and Roman eras, and housed a book shop and auditorium. Having paid the entrance fee, I was free to wander the site at my leisure. Using the map provided, I tried to keep my bearings to understand the topology. I could see how the ruins covered a narrow

Les Antiques, Cenotaph

valley running north to south. The northern part of the town was residential with large villas and baths; the central section was filled with the municipal buildings—the basilica, the curia, the theatre, and temples—with a forum in the center. A stone slab walkway, which turned out to be the cover for the main sewer, wound through the center of the full length of the town. The southern section, the oldest section dating from the time of the pre-Roman Celts, was devoted to the sacred spring of healing waters, the *raison d'etre* for Glanum's existence.

The story of Glanum reaches back to the start of the historical era of Gaul. In the sixth century BC, the earliest inhabitants, the Salluvians, a Celto-Ligurian tribe, built the first small dry-stone dwellings clustered around the sacred spring, which they dedicated to their Celtic god Glanis and his benevolent companions, the Glanic Mothers. As an *oppidum*, this was unusual in that the Salluvians built not on a hilltop as *oppida* elsewhere, but in a valley. They fortified Glanum with the ramparts built on the ridges above the valley, and built a strong gate at the south entrance, which still stands near the sacred spring. When the Greeks established trading centers in the Rhône Valley, they saw the commercial value of Glanum on a pass through the Alpilles for controlling trade routes from ancient Marseille to ancient Avignon, and the town grew and prospered in the second and first centuries BC. The Roman era started in the early years of the reign of Augustus, and the town was given status as an *oppidum latinum*, granting Roman citizenship with full civic and political rights to the local dignitaries. Following the tradition of civic responsibility of Roman nobility, the wealthy patricians of Glanum embellished the town with a building program of grand municipal structures of marble and impressive private houses. During this time the *gens Julii* paid for the construction of the mausoleum at the northern entrance of Glanum.

Glanum did not escape the barbaric invasions of the third century AD; the people were forced to abandon the site and founded a new settlement north of the town that is now St-Remy-de-Provence. In the fourth and fifth centuries AD, the stones of the fine Roman buildings were hauled off, making Glanum a sort of stone quarry, the fate of so many other Roman sites in the South of France and indeed all over the former empire. The edifices that remained were gradually covered over by a thick layer of silt that filled the valley from the erosion of the surrounding hills until the only structures left above the surface were *Les Antiques*. References to Glanum were found in a few medieval records, but after 1260 nothing more is heard of the town. In 1921 French archaeologists rediscovered Glanum from bits of pottery sherds and coins that would turn up periodically, and they conducted excavations over the next twenty years. Today the archaeological work is mainly conservation and restoration, with the numerous artifacts from Glanum housed in the *Hôtel de Sade* in St-Remy for public exhibition.

I spent the afternoon walking the full length of the ancient site and reading the placards. Whenever possible, I would slip into a tour and try to overhear the French tour guide, thought I caught only about ten percent of what was said. Yet I had no trouble getting the feel of the town, the way the people lived, their culture. I was startled to read the name "Agrippa" on an altar stone in front of the Temple of Valetudo next to the Sacred Spring. I found out later that, indeed, Agrippa had the temple built when he was in Gaul from 39 to 37 BC and dedicated it to the Roman goddess of health, Valetudo. Perhaps this temple was an example of religious syncretism combining the Roman Valetudo with the worship of the beneficent Glanic Mothers of the indigenous Celts, whose shrine was just across the road from the Sacred Spring. It occurred to me that this ancient Gallic-Hellenic-Roman site neatly encapsu-

lated the cultural evolution of Provence, at least up to the time of
Germanic invasions.

Walking back to the car park, I spotted a series of placards
scattered in the adjacent wheat field and walked over to investi-
gate. Above the crest of the hill, I could see the roof and tower of
what turned out to be the *Monastère de St. Paul de Mausole*, a hospital
where the Dutch Impressionist painter Vincent Van Gogh spent a
year convalescing from a period of mental illness. The signs in the
fields were copies of his paintings that he did over the year from
1889 to 1890, such as *Cypress Trees* and *The Sower*; the signs were
placed approximately where Van Gogh had set up his easel to paint
the scene. I walked around the dirt path to each sign, noting the
scene as it looks today and how it was rendered by Van Gogh. Not
a lot has changed; the feeling of timelessness had been reinforced.
I knew I would need to make a separate excursion to St-Remy-de-
Provence and also to the famous Van Gogh Museum in Arles.

With daylight fading in the valley, I reluctantly returned to the
car park for the drive home, yet I was filled with a warm satisfac-
tion, as if I had connected with the past, which was my purpose.

I thought over what I had observed at Nîmes, *Pont du Gard*,
and Glanum: the evidence of civilization, the work of generation
and corruption, progress and regression, the destruction and restoration. These are the processes of civilization that are observable,
where humanity has been present for many centuries, where Man
the Builder has been active over many ages, neatly encapsulated in
this region.

That vacation ended all too soon. My three-week experiment
had concluded, with success, I believed. I had demonstrated to
myself that I could navigate my way alone, and complete my goals
of exploring the antiquities of southern France. When it was time

to leave the village and return to Colorado, I packed my belongings, locked up the house, and headed back to Nice for the flight home. Along with my luggage, I carried my observations, grateful for what I had seen and experienced in the warm summer days and I happily anticipated my return the next summer to continue my explorations.

CHAPTER 8

One for the Road

Lyon Airport — The 45th Parallel — The Popes in Avignon — Visit to Carcasonne — Looking for Oppida Undiscovered

Spring was slowly unwrapping in the Rocky Mountains. It had been a cold, harsh winter; the bulbs were putting out tentative shoots in the garden, and the leaves seemed to be reluctant to appear on the tree branches. I was getting that familiar feeling of wanderlust that I get every spring, so I purchased airline tickets for the South of France. I decided to try a different approach. Instead of flying into Nice on the *Côte d'Azur*, which must be followed with the four-hour drive to the Cèze Valley, I would try the airport in Lyon, which might reduce by half the time to get to the village and the house below the château. As the circled travel dates on my calendar approached, the anticipation was sweet. At last, my departure date arrived, and I was again on the road.

The flight leaving the States was delayed by an hour, and the time between my connections in Frankfurt was only an hour and a half. Desperate to make my flight to Lyon, I ran all the way to the gate (Frankfurt is a huge airport) and was rewarded with compliments from the Lufthansa staff on my speed; no one else transferring to Lyon from my flight had made it. I wasn't so sure whether my luggage had made the transfer, but later was happily surprised to see my suitcase at the Lyon airport.

Flying the lower-altitude commuter route from Frankfurt to Lyon over southern Germany and Switzerland gave me a closer view of the Alps. Views over central Europe may not be as spectacular as seeing the blue-green Mediterranean coast at Nice, but it was interesting to trace the Rhône River emerging from the Alps and view the cities that line the river. I could clearly see the beautiful city of Geneva in Switzerland and Lake Geneva with the Rhône entering at the east and exiting from the west. Lyon, called the second city of France, is the site of the confluence of the Rhône flowing west out of the Alps and the Saône flowing from the north, and has been a strategic military and commercial site for centuries. The airport outside Lyon, Saint-Exupéry, is clean, efficient, and has a TGV train station just steps outside the door—useful information I filed away for future trips. Climbing into my rental car and setting the GPS for the village, I was off.

The A7 highway south to Marseilles, called *Autoroute du Soleil*, the Motorway of the Sun, was crowded with commuters, huge trucks hauling heavy goods, and a convoy of brightly painted vehicles from a local circus. The winding *autoroute* crossed and re-crossed the Rhône. I would be travelling only about half of its three hundred kilometer distance, exiting just south of Montélimar. This route through the Rhône Valley has an ancient history; it was used by the army of Julius Caesar in his campaigns against the Helvetians and other Gallic tribes in the first century BC, by invading Saracens in the eighth century AD, and by WWII American GIs in the twentieth. The major cities I passed had cultural signs displaying each city's specialty, and I was intrigued to see the sign for Vienne showing Roman ruins. I found out later that Vienne had been a major Roman city and still contained a fine Corinthian temple built by the Emperor Claudius and dedicated to the memory of Augustus and his wife, Livia, who had been Claudius's grandmother. Claudius had been born in Lyon in 10 BC, while his father, Drusus, was the military commander and administrator of Gaul. Many years ago I read the two-volume historical novel by Robert Graves, *I, Claudius* and *Claudius the God*, which I found absolutely fascinating, and I still have a soft spot in my heart for Claudius. I resolved to return one day and visit Vienne.

Just south of Valence, I passed an exit labeled *Aire de Pont de l'Isere / Latitude 45* and realized at 45 degrees north latitude, I was halfway between the equator and the North Pole—that is, if the earth were a perfect sphere, which it is not. It also occurred to me that the latitude of southern France, with its reputation for bright sunshine, mild winters, verdant fields and vineyards, olive groves, and the occasional palm tree, was about as far north as Fargo, North Dakota. One does not think of Fargo as associated with the wine industry; it has a climate few would regard as sunny and mild and palm trees are unseen except in the botanical gardens. So what makes the climate of Lyon, France, and Fargo, North Dakota, so different? The Mediterranean Sea—that huge, land-locked mass of water with its warm currents isolated from the ocean and trapped between the Straits of Gibraltar to the west and the Straits of the Bosporus to the east. The Mediterranean is the strongest influence on the climate in all the lands that border its coasts.

The British historian G. M. Trevelyan stated, "History is governed by geography." If that is true, France's geographical position on the Western European peninsula provides amazingly beneficial environmental conditions that have proved most conducive to human habitation. Just looking at a world map shows France perched above the Iberian Peninsula, bordered by the Mediterranean Sea and the Atlantic Ocean, enjoying the benefits of the Mediterranean climate and the warming Atlantic Gulf Stream. The physical formation of France and its position on the peninsula of Europe is key to the history of its human settlement and development into its current nation state. I could imagine how the Goths and the Franks, when they happened upon these lands, realized the advantages of the mild climate and the long growing season, and decided to stay. Driving south on the *Autoroute du Soleil*, I had the same feeling.

After crossing the bridge over the Rhône at Pont St. Esprit, I found myself in familiar territory and followed the road signs and roundabouts to Bagnols-sur-Cèze, arriving at the village in the late afternoon. I had enough daylight left to open the house, put away some things, put clean sheets on my bed, and pop in to Bagnols for a few groceries, all of which convinced me that the Lyon route to reach the village outshines the Nice route for practicality.

Feeling at home and quite used to the surroundings, I easily slipped back into my daily routines of baguettes and tea for breakfast, followed by an excursion to shop or explore. By now I had covered all my chosen destinations that were close at hand; I would have to cover greater distances now to reach yet unvisited sites. This seemed like a good time to try the French rail system, and I pictured myself relaxing in a comfy train seat watching the changing landscape, instead of spending hours fighting traffic and getting lost on the national roads. Checking the map for likely destinations, I decided to make a day trip to Carcassonne, reportedly one of the best-preserved medieval walled cities in France and a mere three-hour journey by train.

According to the rail schedule and train pass I bought before leaving the United States, I would have to depart on any train trip from the *Gare Centrale* or the *Gare TGV* in Avignon, which was the closest main station. So the next morning I drove into Avignon to pick up my train reservations for Carcassonne.

༄ ༅

People often ask me what is the nearest large city to our village, and I answer Avignon, a city that is generally known and recognized internationally. Of course, technically, because Avignon is on the east side of the Rhône in the Vaucluse *Département* of Provence, and our village is in the Gard *Département* of Languedoc, they are separate administratively. But in reality the whole region is historically and culturally tied to the story of Avignon.

As with Nîmes, Arles, and Orange, Avignon had its Gallo-Celtic and Roman period, although not much is left of the Roman city. Avignon was captured and occupied by the Saracen Moors from 734 to 737 AD, at which time Charles Martel embarked on his campaigns to drive the Moors out of Provence. In doing so, the ancient river port city of Avignon and its Roman structures were destroyed, and the city fell into decline. Incursions by the Visigoths, Burgundians, and finally Franks all left their mark, but the event that put Avignon on the map, so to speak, was in 1309 when Pope Clement V and the Papal Court abandoned Rome and moved to Avignon.

During the early medieval period, Avignon had held special status as a "commune" under the counts of Provence, independent of the kings of France as well as the Holy Roman Empire. In 1285 Philip IV, *le Bel*, became king of France and ushered in a period of conflict between the kings of France and the popes in Rome. Grandson of the sainted King Louis IX and notorious for his suppression of the Knights Templar in 1307 with the confiscation of their vast wealth, Philip IV saw himself as guardian of his kingdom and special defender of the Roman papacy. Ironically, he fulfilled the second of these two missions by taxing the clergy to raise funds for his wars. Not surprisingly, Pope Boniface VIII reacted with hostility at this violation of papal authority. But before Philip would let Boniface issue a writ of excommunication, one of Philip's henchmen kidnapped Boniface, the shock of which resulted in the elderly pope's death about a month later. After the brief reign of Benedict XI, which came to a suspicious end after eight months, Philip was able to force the election in 1304 of the French archbishop of Bordeaux Bertrand de Got, who took the name Clement V. This was not the first nor the last time a secular ruler intervened in a papal election. It seemed Philip had achieved his goal to

Papal Palace, Avignon

claim supreme power in western Christendom, perhaps enough power even to challenge the Holy Roman Empire. The lynchpin of Philip's power was control of the papacy, which he maintained by keeping the popes geographically close to the French kingdom. He persuaded Pope Clement V to refuse to reside at the Lateran Palace, which Clement publicly justified by stating he preferred to remain in France away from the conflicts, riots, and upheavals in Rome, probably not too far from the truth. In 1309 Clement chose independent Avignon to set up the papal court, the Curia, the Holy See, and centralize the administration of the Catholic Church, making Avignon the power center of western Christendom and the King of France the focus of that power. For the next sixty-eight years, seven popes ruled from Avignon, all French and all answerable to the will of the French kings. In 1348 Pope Clement VII purchased the city from Queen Jeanne of Provence for eighty thousand florins—about sixteen million dollars in today's economy—and Avignon remained papal property until the French Revolution.

With power, prestige, and wealth, the construction of the great Gothic papal palaces began with the building of the Old Palace of Benedict XII from 1334 to 1342 and the New Palace of Clement VI between 1342 and 1352. The buildings were immense, more like fortresses with thick, high walls pierced with narrow openings, massive pointed arches, and huge machicolated battlements and turrets that made them almost impregnable. The interiors were lavishly furnished, full of costly decorations, frescoes, carpets, and tapestries to give the appearance of a regal court. The treasures and luxuries of the Avignon papacy, along with the corruption and venality of the courtiers, became a source of contempt and bitter resentment for the Italians of the old papal court. The poet and humanist Plutarch, who had moved with his family to Avignon to serve Clement V, detested the Avignon papacy, calling it the Second Babylon Captivity, a vicious insult to Avignon when you remember what Babylon was called in the Old Testament. After years of pleading by return-to-Rome supporters such as St. Catherine of Siena, Pope Gregory XI finally made the move back to Rome in 1377. He found Rome a ruined city with perhaps twenty thousand miserable inhabitants huddled in squalor and the Lateran Palace desecrated. The once magnificent, powerful city of Rome, which in the third century AD had a population of more than a million, was at its nadir and showed the scars of suffering from years of wars, barbarian sacks, bubonic plague, and famine.

Even after the return of the popes to Rome, where they took up residence in the Vatican palace around old St. Peter's Basilica, the French were not ready to give up ecclesiastical and temporal power to the Italians. So when Gregory XI died and Urban VI was elected in the Conclave of 1378, the rebellious French cardinals elected their own pope, the "antipope" Clement VII, who resumed his papal court at Avignon. Thus started the Great Schism, when two and, later, three popes reigned, which nearly tore apart western Christendom and dangerously weakened the church.

Avignon went into a slow decline after the popes returned to Rome in 1377. Papal legates continued to govern the city after 1417 when the Great Schism was finally resolved, and in 1791 the French National Assembly annexed Avignon. During the French Revolution, the papal palace was seized, resulting in much destruction and bloodshed, and was used as munitions storage and a barracks from 1822 to 1906, which seemed to confirm its original intended function.

All these years later, most people have forgotten the enormous political power the Roman Church wielded in the Middle Ages and the Renaissance. The transformation of Western Europe from Late Antiquity through the Middle Ages and into the Renaissance was primarily a transfer of power from the Roman emperors to the popes, who were the bishops of Rome and became very like the new Roman emperors with all the trappings of prestige and secular, temporal power. While the various barbarian tribes were dividing and conquering the remnants of the Imperial lands, each with their own leaders, customs, local laws, and languages, the bishops of Rome and the church they represented were the single unifying force. They were the common factor, the authority that enabled Western civilization to survive the early Middle Ages. The educated clergy became indispensable in the courts and governments of the secular leaders because the clergy could read and write, making Latin the *lingua franca* of Europe until the eighteenth century. One interesting side-note: the language of the early Christian church was Greek, not Latin, and only became Latin after Roman Emperor Theodosius the Great proclaimed Christianity the state religion in 391. Greek was the *lingua franca* of the ancient world, and every well-educated Roman was taught Greek.

The concept of a "nation" was a nineteenth-century construct, following the French Revolution and Napoleonic Wars. People of the Middle Ages identified themselves as citizens of their native city rather than as Italian or German or French. According to British historian G. M. Trevylan, the only name by which Europe of the Middle Ages knew itself was Christendom, and its only capital was Papal Rome. The popes controlled a vast swath of land in the central Italian peninsula, called the Papal States, which they claimed from the ancient Donation of Constantine—later proved to be a forgery—and guarded their territory with papal armies. The militant Pope Julius II, who persuaded Michelangelo to paint the ceiling of the Sistine Chapel, was the last pope to ride into battle in 1506 during the Italian Wars. The temporal power of the papacy ended in 1870 with the unification of Italy into a nation, which deprived the papacy of the Papal States, and Pius XI, the pope at the time, retreated into the Vatican under protest. The Lateran Treaty of 1929, a gesture of appeasement from the fascist government of

Vittorio Emmanuel III and Benito Mussolini to Pope Pius XI to make up for the loss of papal territory and sovereignty, created the Vatican State.

ɷ ɷ

Speeding eastbound over the bridge crossing the Rhône, I beheld the medieval skyline of Avignon to the north. Avignon, once the center of power of Western Christendom and having survived papal abandonment, still has its machicolated towers and fortress walls, which are reflected in the waters of the Rhône. Upstream a little way, one could see the four remaining arches of the Pont-St-Bénézet, the twelfth-century Bridge of Avignon that is the subject of a French children's' song: *"Sur le pont d'Avignon, l'on y danse, l'on y danse. . ."* "On the bridge of Avignon we will dance, we will dance..." That song runs through my head every time I cross the bridge over the Rhône at Avignon.

Remembering the city's history, I'm always amazed at how well Avignon has adapted and joined the modern world. The main train station, the *Gare Central SNCF,* is at the southern end of the walled city. Wanting to make a short walking tour, I parked there and entered into the *centre ville* through the massive stone gates. Walking along the main axis, the *Rue de la République,* I reached the central shopping area, which is a pedestrian-only zone. The area contains an impressive variety of fashionable stores, some of which are branches of the Parisian originals, and charming shops with Provençal specialties, including a shop that sells lovely Provençal tableware and ceramics. Near the commercial zone is a neighborhood of Gothic mansions, which I presumed were the townhomes that had been built centuries ago for the members of the papal Curia.

The heart of the city is the main square on the *Rue de la République* called the *Place de l'Horloge* that was once the Roman forum of Avignon. The square is lined with outdoor cafés, a large carousel for the kids, the imposing theatre, and the *Hôtel de Ville*, built during the Second Empire and attached to the Gothic *Tour de l'Horloge*, the old clock tower, a remnant of an ancient convent. At the northern tip of the walled city is the *Jardin du Rocher des Doms*, the picturesque greenery of the city park. Here, legend has it, Augustus wanted to construct a temple dedicated to the god Boreas, the North Wind, on the highest point of the city. The view from the park is breathtaking: the Rhône shimmering at the edge of the city walls with multiple bridges spanning it, and on the opposite bank the tower of Philip IV, *le Bel*, and the city of Villeneuve-les-Avignon. To the northeast are the distant slopes of Mont Ventoux, looking the same as when Petrarch climbed the mountain in 1336 while he was living in Avignon. But the real attraction for the visitor is, of course, the *Palais des Papes*, the Palace of the Popes. One can only imagine what it must have been like at the time of the papal court with the halls crowded with princes, cardinals, clergymen, and courtiers, as well as all the Italian and French artists at that time, the dawn of the Renaissance. Just south of the palace is the cathedral of Avignon, *Notre-Dame des Doms*, an imposing Romanesque-style church with a square bell tower topped with a golden statue of the Virgin Mary. The building dates from the twelfth century, but the site has had a church since the fourth century. According to legend, a church on this spot was founded by St. Martha in honor of the Virgin. The elegant *Notre-Dame des Doms* seems to soften the stark austerity of the papal palace next to it.

Every year in July the spectacles of the Festival of Avignon are held in the huge courtyard in front of the palace. This arts festival began in 1947 and has become one of the most important theatre and performance arts festivals in Europe. For the three weeks of the festival, which involves hundreds of performances, the city is crammed with visitors.

After an enjoyable stroll through Avignon's city center, I made my way back to the main train station and arranged my reservations for the three trains I would need to catch for Carcassonne.

ᏨᏙ ᏙᏫ

Waking up very early the next morning, I skipped breakfast and made my way to Avignon in complete darkness. The trains in France run amazingly on time, so I made it a point to arrive at the station with plenty of breathing room before the 0630 departure. The predawn air was a bit chilly but would become quite warm by midday, so I dressed in layers and carried my trusty canvas tote. I boarded the first regional train with no trouble and found a seat from where I could watch the countryside change from the rolling greenery of the Rhône Valley to the sparsely populated lowlands south of the forested hills of the *Montagne Noire*, the Black Mountains.

At the first transfer, I eagerly jumped off the train onto the station platform and thought I'd look for the restrooms. Regretting not having availed myself of the restroom when I was on board the train, I followed the signs through the main station, out a side door, and, adjacent to a loading dock, and found what seemed to be a double-wide plastic "port-o-potty." Hardly an inviting rest stop, I thought, figuring that by now I had seen everything in the way of French toilet accommodations. The coin-operated latch would not take my coins, but I continued to try until a lady appeared, having also followed the signs.

"Is this it?" she asked incredulously with a distinctly Scottish accent.

One for the Road

"I think so, but my coins keep falling out, and I can't get the door to open." She noted my desperate frustration and fished into her purse for some coins.

"Try these," she offered, and they worked like magic. I held open the door for her to go in first, and while I waited, I read the posted signs on the plastic sides of the port-o-potty. One notice stated in English: "This restroom is sanitized after each use." Whatever could that mean? The Scots lady emerged and held the door open for me.

"No use in you wasting your 30 cents," she said as she disappeared back into the train station. Her logic seemed reasonable to me at the time.

However, as soon as I closed the door, the lights switched off—the first indication that this would not be a happy potty stop. *Ah, I thought, this is programmed to admit only one paying customer at a time.* As I groped around in the darkness looking for the business section, I heard a sharp hissing at the floor level. What's that? Suddenly I felt water being sprayed over the floor; I was so startled that I tried dancing around on tiptoe to avoid the sprays and getting soaked. Nope, my hiking shoes and jeans halfway up to my knees were quickly sodden, and it dawned on me the meaning of the sign "This restroom is sanitized after each use." Yuck.

After the spraying stopped, I managed to complete what I came for, trying to keep my things off the soaking wet floor. I reached for the door, but it wouldn't open. I felt around the door for a latch, a sign—anything—and the image flashed in my mind of being trapped for hours in this plastic French train station outhouse. Instantly panicking, I started to pound on the door, calling for help in French. "*Aidez-moi, s'il vous plaît!*" Nothing. After what seemed like forever but was probably only five minutes, my eyes adjusted to the dark, and I spotted a large red circle to the left of the door. I touched it and found it was a button! Aha! Upon pushing it, the door popped open. Sweet freedom! As I exited, I glanced around to see if anyone had witnessed my disgraceful behavior. Shoes squishing, I nonchalantly walked to my train and boarded, trying to maintain that air of *je ne sais quoi*, but looking as though I had just waded through a shallow pool. Okay, lesson learned. From now on, don't forget to use the restrooms on board the trains.

❧ ❧

Pulling into the train station at Carcassonne, in the new part of the city called *Ville Basse*, Lower Town, and also referred to as *Bastide de St. Louis*, I jumped off and set out for what I thought would be a short walk up to the medieval citadel perched on a bluff above the *Ville Basse*. I passed a small boat dock that advertised rides on the *Canal du Midi*, the skillfully engineered canal built in the seventeenth century to link the Mediterranean and the Atlantic, covering a distance of 240 kilometers and varying elevations with ninety-one locks. Jean-Baptiste Colbert, the finance minister of King Louis XIV, approved the funds for construction of the canal, which allowed for freight transportation across southern France and avoided the long and dangerous sea voyage around the Iberian Peninsula. The port on the canal at Carcassonne connects the barge system with the regional train system for passenger and cargo transport. Pleasure cruises have always been popular, and the boat dock had some houseboats as well as barges. Consulting the map, which indicated the walk up to the medieval city would take about thirty minutes, I decided to save time and take a shuttle bus up to the citadel.

For years I have dreamed of visiting this city, a UNESCO World Heritage site, and as the shuttle bus came in sight of the medieval towers and walls, I wondered why it took me so long to get here.

Carcassonne is probably Languedoc's best-known landmark and favorite tourist destination with its thick machicolated rampart walls almost three kilometers around, barbicans, moats and drawbridges, and fifty towers with grey cones on top. It began as a Celtic *oppidum* in the fifth century BC and then became a Roman fortress in the second century AD, which was taken over by the Visigoths. Later its relative isolation became a haven for the Cathars of the eleventh century. The *Cité Médiévale* dates from the twelfth century and survived the Cathar wars as well as the turbulent Middle Ages. The crumbling remains were restored under the direction of the Parisian architect Eugène Viollet-le-Duc in the nineteenth century. The reconstruction was not without criticism, however. Viollet-le-Duc used gray slate for the conical roofs instead of terra-cotta tiles to cover the towers, giving the restored Carcassonne a decidedly northern French appearance. I was willing to overlook that and began exploring.

After walking through the main gate, *La Porte Narbonnaise*, I found myself engulfed in a swarm of tourists, all squeezing through the narrow medieval streets, looking for trinkets in the souvenir shops and snapping pictures. This could be the set of some Robin Hood movie. I found out later that Carcassonne has indeed been used for medieval sets in recent films. The shops seemed determined to preserve the crafts of the Middle Ages, with authentic clothing, shoes, bonnets, tapestries, and medieval weaponry toys filling the window displays. Again and again I saw the Cathar Cross and the Cross of Languedoc emblazoned on flags, postcards, ceramics, and refrigerator magnets. The chalkboards outside the cafés all listed *cassoulet* on the daily menu, a savory casserole of pork, sausage, duck, goose, and white beans, the traditional dish of southwest France, among other tasty delights. Outside of a small museum called *Memoires du Moyen Age*, Memories of the Middle Ages, stood a life-size figure of a crusader and a scale model of a bricole, a stone-hurling catapult for bombarding fortresses just like Carcassonne.

Carcassonne - *Château Comtal*

I walked to the end of the lane and found *Château Comtal*, the Castle of the Viscounts, a magnificent medieval castle that had been the home of the Trencavel family, vassals to the counts of Toulouse. A line of tourists just like me waited to get a photo of the castle from a particular spot, a classic view of the barbican with the moat and stone bridge that appears on postcards in all the shops.

Trying to remember the history, I recalled that the Trencavels, as well as Count Raymond V of Toulouse, all lost their lands when the armies of Simon de Montfort and the king of France crushed the Cathars during the Albigensian Crusades in the early 1200s. Carcassonne's massive walls resisted assault by de Montfort's armies, but the city fell to the crusaders after a negotiated truce. I wondered how many tourists relaxing at the outdoor cafés were aware of what had happened on these streets eight hundred years ago.

Wandering south, I came upon the marvelous Gothic church, *La Basilique Saint-Nazaire*. The earliest parts of the building date from the sixth century under the reign of Theodoric, King of the Visigoths, and in the twelfth century was replaced by a Romanesque building, of which only the nave remains. The Gothic arcades and choir and the stained-glass rose windows were added in the thirteenth and fourteenth centuries, and after restoration, again by Viollet-le-Duc in the nineteenth century, we have this wonderful example of medieval French Gothic architecture. While I was inside *Saint-Nazaire*, a male quartet performed haunting Gregorian polyphonic music. Beautiful ancient music in a perfect medieval setting—it was one of those moments that created a treasured memory for me.

After giving in to the temptations of all those souvenir shops, I caught the shuttle bus outside the walls and made it back to the train station in time to catch my train back to Avignon. From one medieval walled city to another. On the train I started thinking of how much better I was getting at recognizing architectural styles of buildings and associating them with a good estimate of the age. With a little effort, an alert observer of architecture in southern France can find examples that run the gamut from six thousand-year-old dolmens in the forest to the ultra-modern *Carré d'Art* in Nîmes by the famous British architect Norman Foster. I could easily spot the remnants of Roman buildings, from temples to amphitheatres, and I was able to see how features of the Roman architecture had been converted into the Neoclassical style, such as in the Pantheon in Paris.

The architecture of the early Middle Ages is generally called Romanesque and is distinguished by rounded arches, small windows, and heavy walls. What followed and what started in France, in an inexplicable leap of architectural engineering, was called Gothic in the sixteenth century by the Germans who wished to denigrate it, Gothic meaning barbaric. The earliest Gothic building is said to be the abbey cathedral of *St. Denis* in Paris, dating from about 1135 under the direction of the Abbot Suger. The Gothic style introduced by Suger, perhaps invented by him, has the characteristic pointed arches and flying buttresses to better distribute weight and stress of the walls, allowing for tall windows filled with stained glass, and ribbed vault interiors that seemed to soar into the sky. Abbot Suger, an extraordinary individual of twelfth century France, was an unapologetic lover of art and beauty, and believed the mind of man could rise to the heavens through the appreciation of beauty. The French Gothic became the dominant style of northern Europe for the next five hundred years and was adopted in Germany, England, Spain, and northern Italy for both church and secular public buildings. At the start of the Italian Renaissance, a newer architectural style emerged from Tuscany, centered in Florence, and was associated with the great architects Brunelleschi, Bramante, and Palladio in the mid-fifteenth and early sixteenth century. The Counter-Reformation in the sixteenth century brought with it the Baroque, the exuberant and flamboyant style that, along with it the even more excessive Rococo, signifies the reaction against Protestantism and rigid classicism. Rococo is easy to spot because of the over-the-top plaster decorations using swirling vines, fruits, flowers, cupids, and seashells, which is the origin of the name "rococo" —*coquille* means shell.

Each architectural style carries an associated message. I remember the first time I visited Washington, DC, and was impressed with the number of Neoclassical white, marble buildings, such as that perfect Roman temple called the Supreme Court building. I think the selection of Neoclassicism as the architectural style used to design the capital city of the United States was a conscious decision. Called the Federal style, Neoclassicism imparts a sense of strength and stability recalling the Roman Republic. I'm sure the Founding Fathers, steeped in the rational philosophy of the eighteenth century Enlightenment, used it to convey to European heads of state the message that the new Republic of the United States was for real. In contrast, after a disastrous fire in 1834 the Palace of Westminster and Houses of Parliament in London were rebuilt in the Gothic-revivalist style, again with a specific message: that of nineteenth century British conservatism and monarchism. Architecture as a tool of politics.

It was almost dark when my final connecting train pulled into *Gare Centrale SNCF* outside the walls of Avignon. I paid my parking ticket at the kiosk and drove back to the village feeling a satisfying mixture of exhaustion and contentment.

∽ ⌇

Between train trips, I finally found time for the bit of fun I had been putting off for far too long: to locate the ancient *oppidum* that the curator of the *Maison de Patrimonie et Histoire* told me was hidden in the wooded hills above the village. I looked at my well-worn maps, now dog-eared and marked with scribbled notes, and found the penciled "X" where she guessed it might be found. I remember her mentioning *sangliers*, wild boars, in the woods as one reason she had not made the hike herself, and I wondered if I should be worried. Undaunted, probably because this would be my last chance to try to find it on this trip, I set out after lunch with my map, water bottle, and sturdy walking stick in case I encountered any snakes or wild boars.

The sunny afternoon grew warm as I walked along the dirt road past the château to the mountain summit above the village. I turned at a crossroad and headed into a small valley with the usual field of grapevines. No sign of who the field belonged to or any workers. I continued on that path as it rose in elevation toward another summit. The curator had called this *Mont Barri*, a spur of exposed limestone rock topped with the green shrubs of the *garrigue*. Ascending to the summit, which was about three hundred meters altitude, I was shaded in the canopy of trees above the winding dirt path, which dimmed the sunlight, and I soon became disoriented. After walking for about forty-five minutes, I spotted a jumble of stones that looked like they had been placed by man instead of by nature. Hmmm, can this be the edge of a wall of the *oppidum*? I had no way of knowing if I had reached the summit, but started poking around in the brambles next to the path. In the gloom I could make out a course of eroded stones covered with moss that seemed to define sections of a low wall. The course continued on the other side of the path, and within the grove of slender trees and tangle of vines, I could see more mossy stones. In my best Indiana Jones imitation, I tromped through the thick brush to the stones and detected what looked like foundations to four buildings, roughly rectangular, with the highest section of stones reaching about a meter above the surface. There were more pieces of the mossy stone wall that could have once defined a large enclosed area. With so much vegetation and so little light, I couldn't see much more and returned to the path, twig-scratched and brushing dried leaves from my hair. Was this it? The curator had told me the *oppidum* dated from 2000 BC. Is that possible? Could this pile of stones hidden in the forest be that old? Neolithic pottery sherds had also been found around there. I remembered reading about how a funerary stele with a Latin inscription had been found in the woods above the village and wondered if this was the site.

I trudged back to the house to make dinner, my mind filled with questions about my discovery. If only I knew who owned the land on which I saw all those mossy stones, I could find out if anyone really knew the true age and purpose of that site. Just that quick look at what might be an ancient site in its natural state, untouched for perhaps hundreds of years, gave me renewed appreciation and respect for the hard work real archaeologists must do to conduct scientific excavations. The thought of excavating the site on what I guessed was the *oppidum* of the village looked like an enormous, multi-year task. Would I like to be part of it? Oh, yes, in a heartbeat!

CHAPTER 9

Church and State in France

**The Abbey Church in Goudargues — The Cathars —
The Huguenots — The Religious Wars —Legacy of
Enlightenment and Revolution — Laïcité**

I n southern France, and indeed all over Central and Western
Europe, there are still religious monuments of traditional
Christian piety in public places. Our village has two examples
of large wrought iron crucifixes set in stone pedestals that have
stood in the small plazas for centuries and are maintained by
the municipality at public expense. It seems every village has
such crosses as well as small wayside shrines with statues of the
Virgin Mary, St. Joseph, St. Martin of Tours, or other saints,
which have been carefully tended, sometimes containing vases
of fresh flowers. The intersection of the main road and the
turnoff to our village has a large concrete cross, which I find
very useful as a landmark. Each town or village has its church

with spires or a bell tower, and it is often the tallest building in town. I was pleasantly surprised to hear the bells in our village church chime the Angelus (three sets of three rings followed by ten quick rings) at eight o'clock in the morning, noon, and seven o'clock in the evening to signify when the faithful should recite special prayers to the Virgin Mary.

I was not unfamiliar or uncomfortable with these traditional displays of ancient Roman Catholic piety. However, as an American who was raised on the inviolate principle of the separation of church and state, it was clear my understanding of the French concept of secularization needed some work.

∾ ∾

Sunday was approaching, and I checked the notice board outside the village church to see in which of the surrounding villages Sunday Mass would be held. In this region, as in many places, church attendance has dwindled to the point that Masses are said for the combined congregations of several villages, and the locations are on a rotating schedule: Montclus, St. Laurent de Carnols, Verfeuil, Goudargues, St. Michel d'Euzet, St. Sauveur, and Sabran. I decided to attend the next Sunday Mass, which was scheduled to be at Goudargues.

I awoke with the Angelus bells at eight o'clock Sunday morning and, after a cup of tea and baguette, set off for Goudargues. It is only about a fifteen-minute drive west of our village and is also on the Cèze River. It is conveniently close for quick grocery trips or to pick up goodies at the *boulangerie*.

This was my second try to attend Mass in Goudargues. During my visit last summer, I was disappointed in my initial attempt

Abbey church in Goudargues

because, unsure of the Mass time, I arrived just as people were leaving. But the church was still open, and I took a few minutes to look around the interior. I found on the back wall a faded poster board detailing a little history of the building that had been excerpted from the *Dictionary of Ecclesiastical History and Geography* by R. Aubert, printed in Paris in 1960. It related the story of how the church was originally part of an abbey, a Benedictine monastery, founded by William II, Count of Toulouse, born in 755 and who was a grandson on his mother's side of Charles Martel, and so was a cousin to Charlemagne. William was a military commander in the wars of the Carolingian Franks against the invading Moorish Saracens and had served in the army when the Franks recovered Barcelona in 802. However, in his later years, William was attracted to the monastic life probably because of his friendship with St. Benedict of Aniane, called 'the second Benedict' to distinguish him from St Benedict of Nursia, the author of the monastic Benedictine Rule. Encouraged by Charlemagne to spread Benedictine monasticism, William founded several monasteries, including this abbey in Goudargues. William died in 812 at his monastery of *St. Guilhem le Desert*, near Aniane, which was a stop on the famed medieval pilgrimage route to St. James Compostela in Spain. I found out later that the cloister of *St. Guilhem le Desert* was purchased by an American sculptor after World War I and is now preserved at the Cloisters of New York Metropolitan Museum of Art. So I would be attending Sunday services in the church that was originally part of an abbey that was founded by a sainted cousin of Charlemagne, whose monastery cloister I had already visited in New York!

I was able to park by the canal behind the church and happily noted the *boulangerie* would be open until 12:30 p.m. so I could buy some fresh bread and pastries after Mass. I had discovered a wonderful pastry here called a *sacristain*, I suppose in honor of the ancient monastery, and hoped the supply would hold out for another hour.

Entering the church, I felt the coolness of the interior due to the thick stone walls, dipped my fingers into the holy water in the large, carved stone fountain, and selected a seat. The church looked as if it could hold about one hundred people, but today there were only about thirty, and of those, only two young families.

The interior decorations were almost absent; the walls of the nave were bare plaster instead of frescoes, and there were only a few statues. The stone floors had the well-worn look of centuries of use, and the raised floors of the side chapels contained faded mosaics. The walls of the apse at the front were painted and decorated with stone statues, which gave me some idea of what the rest may have looked like centuries before. The history posted in the back of the church had mentioned the damage suffered by the building at the hands of the Cathars during the Albigensian Crusade from 1214 to 1230 and subsequent damage inflicted by the Huguenots during the Religious Wars of 1570 to 1590. I wondered whether the reduced number of statues and bare walls was lingering evidence of the iconoclasm of those wars.

The air was fragrant from the lavender and hydrangea bouquets that decorated the altar in the side chapel near me. Soon, however, the cool interior grew close with the presence of the faithful. The choir, singing not quite in tune with the tired organ, was composed of the usual array of senior citizens. The service in French was surprisingly easy for me to follow; the sermon, prayers, and readings were delivered at a fraction of the speed of normal conversation. I felt at ease singing the responses in French, as the form of the Mass was the same as at home. "Catholic" comes from the Greek word *katholikos*, meaning universal, and the structure of the Mass really is universal, at least from what I have observed in attending Mass in Germany, Italy, England, Australia, and now France.

Walking outside after the service into the bright sunlight, I was greeted with smiles and friendly nods from the other worshippers.

Children skipped up and down the worn stone steps while their parents chatted, and there was a casual procession in the general direction of the *boulangerie*, where a queue had already formed. I was again struck by the fact that I felt so at home and not necessarily in awe for the antiquity of this church and its surroundings. I was quietly thrilled that attending Mass in a church built in the late eighth century felt so natural, so unremarkable. This was not the first time I had experienced that feeling when visiting some ancient and historical spot: the past is so close, almost intimate. The people didn't seem to let the past intrude on the present. The approach seemed to say, there is no need to be awed by the history that always surrounds us; there is still work to be done, so you'd best get on with it. Here the past seems to flow into the present like the calm waters of the Cèze River through Gourdauges, through vineyards and past Bagnols, and into the mighty Rhône, about twenty kilometers to the east.

∽ ᗖ

Driving back to the village after Mass, I remembered the complex and often violent religious history of this country. It occurred to me how the existence of this abbey church was a story of survival. If I had been here in 1214 or 1565, I might not have expected this building to withstand the religious crises that historians now refer to as the Albigensian Crusade or the later Huguenot Wars. These were the two major episodes in French history that pitted the orthodox Roman Catholic powers against the perceived heretics, the Cathars of the twelfth and thirteenth centuries and the Huguenots of the sixteenth. I wondered whether the Religious Wars had been just as important in shaping the character of Provence and Languedoc as was the Roman occupation.

The origin of the Cathars is somewhat murky and still debated by historians. One theory traces the Cathars to a heretical sect that sprung up in the Balkans in the tenth century and moved into Italy and southern France. As with so many reforming religious sects, the Cathars demanded extreme asceticism of their adherents, rejecting all sex and procreation (which made me wonder how they sustained the sect's population), and refraining from eating meat, eggs, milk, or cheese. They rejected all clergy, sacraments, the liturgy, and the saints, and instead of baptism they practiced the laying of hands. The only prayer they accepted was the *paternoster*, the Lord's Prayer. They were "dualists," in that they regarded creation as split in two, an evil physical world and a good spiritual world. Their duality was driven by a basic need to explain the presence of evil in the world. They devised an elaborate mythology to answer their questions: "How can there be evil in a world created by a good God?" and "How can there be good in an evil world?" Satan was the fallen angel, the *Rex Mundi*—the king of the evil material world—and Christ was the king of heaven. Christ's mission on earth was to lead the fallen angles out of the clutches of the Rex Mundi and back to heaven.

The Cathar devotee, called a Perfect, sought to free himself from sin through celibacy and fasting, and avoided soiling his soul by material things. Procreation was seen as the continuation of the world of evil and was shunned. Meat could not be eaten because the animal might have contained the soul of a fallen sinner. With their rejection of the physical world, the Cathars kept to themselves; they formed their own societies, towns, and markets, and generally stayed out of trouble. However, as their numbers grew (presumably from converts) and they spread from northern Italy throughout Languedoc and Provence, they became a threat to the established authority, the Roman Church. They became associated with the town of Albi and thus were called Albigensians, although they were also prominent in Beziers, Carcassonne, Toulouse, and many other smaller towns in southern France. Gradually, the Cathars earned the protection of two rival factions of nobles who competed for control the region, the Counts of Toulouse and the Trencavel family, who were vassals to the kings of Aragon in northern Spain. As the protection by these nobles moved the Cathars from the status of a purely religious community into the realm of politics, they became convenient pawns in a struggle for power and land.

In the second half of the twelfth century, wars between these two noble factions were occasionally interrupted with truces and treaties. Warfare resumed in 1177, with Count Raymond V of Toulouse finding himself on the losing end against the Trencavels and William of Montpellier, who were fighting for Alphonse II of Aragon. In what turned out later to be a strategic blunder, Raymond appealed to the Capet King Louis VIII and the religious Order of Citeaux, the Cistercians, playing on the danger of corruption from the Cathar heresy, to find allies in the north. In this way Raymond brought together the major components of the later crusade, the active intervention of the Cistercians, who instituted an Inquisition against the Cathars, and invasion of Cathar lands by the Capetian army of the King of France. When it was finally over in 1255, the Albigensian Crusade succeeded in bringing down Count Raymond's son along with the Trencavels with the loss of their lands and titles. After that, the Languedoc, which had been independent since the Romans left, became subject to the French Crown.

The initial crusade, which started in 1209 and lasted until 1215, was instigated after the murder of the papal legate Pierre de Castelnau, who had unsuccessfully tried to persuade Count Raymond of Toulouse to abandon his protection of the Cathars. The pope issued a call to the nobles of the north to crusade against the nobles of the south and fight the scourge of heresy. Louis

VIII sent his army, headed by Simon de Montfort, a veteran of the Fourth Crusade in the Holy Land and a man with a reputation for brutality. The conflict was a struggle for power and land ownership between the northern French nobles and the southern Languedocian nobles under the guise of a religious cause. Thus began years of conflict that saw battles, sieges, and massacres. In perhaps the most notorious outrage, the city of Beziers was sacked and burned in 1209, and the entire population was slaughtered—some sources estimate as many as twenty thousand men, women, and children. Town after town was besieged; perhaps the abbey church in Goudargues was damaged during this time. Some towns gave up without a fight after hearing of the terror of Beziers, and the destruction and bloodshed ended in 1215 after the city of Toulouse fell to Simon de Montfort.

The peace was temporary; the nobles and the populace soon reverted to their old ways, and new rebellions broke out. Count Raymond gathered new supporters to regain his territory. But even with the death of Simon de Montfort in 1218, the Cathars and their noble protectors could not prevail against the French army of the king. When it was over in 1255, all of Languedoc was firmly in the control of the French. The Aragonese political control was ended forever. The last Cathar heretic was executed in 1321 in Switzerland, bringing an end to the Cathar heresy. Travelling through Languedoc today, you may see signs announcing this to be *Pays Cathare*, the Land of the Cathars, with residents claiming to be descendants of the Cathars, but I suspect this is mostly for the benefit of the tourist industry. I saw a fair amount of Cathar-themed souvenirs in the shops when I visited Carcassonne.

The history of the Huguenots is somewhat different. The origin of the Religious Wars in sixteenth-century France can be traced to the Protestant Reformation begun by Martin Luther in Germany.

While the Cathars just wanted to be left alone, Luther wanted to reform the Church of Rome and purge it of corruption. When Luther nailed his declaration, known as the "95 Theses," on the door of All Saints Church in Wittenberg in October 1517, he set in motion a great upheaval of power and a redistribution of wealth in Western Christendom, the effects of which surround us today.

Martin Luther (1483–1546), born in Eisleben, Saxony, in what was then the Holy Roman Empire, was a devout Augustinian monk, a scholar and theologian, and the first translator of the Bible into German. His protest in Wittenberg was based on his rejection of the clergy's common practice of the sale of indulgences as a means of raising revenues; in this instance, for the rebuilding of the great Basilica of St. Peter in Rome. The church's long-standing doctrine of indulgences allowed for the relief of temporal punishment to the sinner after the sin was confessed and absolution was granted. Indulgences were usually earned by the sinner through good works and prayer. The corrupt sixteenth-century clergy's eagerness to buy and sell indulgences to exploit an unsophisticated and superstitious laity prompted Luther's call to the peasants of Germany to resist what he saw as a shakedown for salvation, which drained the wealth from the people of Germany to enrich the coffers in Rome.

Luther's protest soon earned him the wrath of the Medici Pope Leo X and the Habsburg Holy Roman Emperor Charles V, but he refused to recant his views at the conference in 1521, called the Diet of Worms. I remember reading a biography of Martin Luther, which was entitled *Here I Stand,* his reported quote in front of the Diet and the statement that marked his permanent breach with the Catholic Church. Luther became a powerful force throughout Germany, probably because of the use of the newly invented printing press that aided the distribution of his writings. However, his message would not have taken hold of the people had the people not been receptive. I think the Reformation couldn't have started anywhere else but Germany, with its tradition of fierce independence, resistance to authority imposed from outside, and the German propensity to tell everyone else how they should live. Luther ignited a reaction in the German spirit, which had lain dormant for generations and became the kernel of the rise of German nationalism many years later. I remember in reading *The Rise and Fall of the Third Reich*, William Shirer made the impressive assertion that Luther's impact on German history could not be overstated. Luther was quickly followed by other messengers of Reformation: Ulrich Zwingli in Switzerland, John Knox in Scotland, and John Calvin in France. And, as with the Cathars, their secular protectors emerged—in this case, the German princes who hoped to gain political autonomy from the Holy Roman Empire and the Church of Rome. Inevitably, the theological dissension led to bloodshed; possibly the first was the German Peasant's Revolt of 1525, with many more to follow. What started as a religious movement quickly accelerated into a struggle for political power.

In 1530 the French theologian Jean Cauvin, known to us as John Calvin, broke away from the Roman Church and instituted another Reformation doctrine that attracted followers in France, who eventually became the Huguenots. John Calvin did for the French Protestants what Luther did for the German Protestants. They called themselves "Reformed" or "Calvinists" but sometime after 1560, seeking political power and influence, acquired the name "Huguenots." Historians believe that they took their name from the port of Hugues near Nantes, the location where they concocted the Amboise Conspiracy, the plot in 1560 to kidnap the Valois King Francois II and to remove the leaders of the ultra-Catholic House of Guise permanently. The plan failed, but the formidable Queen Regent Catherine de Medici used the occasion to broker a truce between the two rival political factions, the House of Bourbon-Navarre, who were Protestant, and the House of Guise, the Catholics.

The Bourbons considered the Guises to be upstarts from Lorraine, greedy for power and influence at court. Their niece, Mary Queen of Scots, was the wife of the French King Francois II, which gave the Guises considerable political clout. On the other hand, the Bourbons were true "Princes of the Blood," having descended directly from King Louis IX. Their leader, Antoine de Bourbon, was married to Jeanne d'Albret, Queen of Navarre, and was the closest heir to the throne after the Valois. To maintain peace, Catherine de Medici skillfully played one faction against the other, favoring one, then the other; her main purpose was the survival of the Valois line on the throne of France. Leaders emerged for each faction: Francois Duke de Guise for the Catholics, and Admiral Gaspard de Coligny, nephew of the Constable of France Anne de Montmorency, for the Huguenot Bourbons. The resulting conflicts, separated into seven wars, were even more blood curdling than the Albigensian Crusades. Presumably the church of the abbey in Goudargues underwent further damage, and the abbey itself was destroyed by the Huguenots. The most infamous outrage is what became known as St. Bartholomew's Day Massacre.

Here again the cause of the conflict was, in reality, political power and land ownership, not religion as they claimed. Coligny had arranged for the assassination of Francois de Guise (the two had been friends in their youth), a power grab that was so alarming to Catherine de Medici that, fearing a Huguenot *coup d'état* to depose her son Charles IX and put Antoine de Bourbon on the throne, she conspired with her third son, Henry Duke d'Anjou, to have Coligny murdered. The occasion was the marriage of her daughter Margaret of Valois (Queen Margot) to Henry of Navarre, the son of Antoine de Bourbon, which was to take place on 24 August 1572, St. Bartholomew's Day. The plan was to eliminate Coligny and the Huguenot leaders who had assembled in Paris for the wedding, but the killing of Coligny and his men escalated into a general attack by the Parisians against the Huguenots—any and all Huguenots. The Parisians broke into their homes and dragged them into the streets to murder them by the hundreds. The uprising spread to other cities—Nîmes, Toulouse, and Rheims—an incomprehensible bloodlust. The killings multiplied so rapidly that it is likely a good many were revenge killings, the settling of old scores, and the elimination of competitors and unwanteds. By the end of the bloodshed in early October 1572, some seventy thousand people had lost their lives.

Incredibly, even after this horrific savagery, the people did not come to their senses and put an end to the wars. Before the last of Catherine de Medici's sons died and the Valois line was extinguished in 1589, France suffered four more outbreaks of violence. When Henry of Navarre, Antoine's son and the Bourbon heir, came to the throne in 1589 as Henry IV, he was warned that he would have to fight for his crown and that the Parisians would never accept a Huguenot king. Seeing the advantage of political expediency, Henry compromised his religious scruples and converted to Catholicism, famously saying, "Paris is well worth a Mass" (*"Paris vaut bien une messe"*).

Henry IV turned out to be a good, brave, and generous king, perhaps the most beloved by his people in all of French history. This first Bourbon king, who was grandfather to both Louis XIV of France and the Stuart King Charles II of England, worked to bring peace, prosperity, and industry to modernize France. I am reminded of the orchard of mulberry trees planted near the *Pont du Gard* at Henry's direction to feed the silkworms to support the silk-making industry that had been introduced into Provence in the fifteenth century. Henry wanted each Frenchman to have "a chicken in every pot" on Sundays *"le dimanche une poule dans sur pot"* a phrase attributed to him centuries before Herbert Hoover during the Depression. He endeavored to end the Wars of Religion by his Edict of Nantes of 1598, which provided for religious toleration, freedom of worship for the Huguenots, and a chance for them to partake in the general prosperity.

Henry's reign was cut short; he was assassinated in 1610 by a fanatic Catholic who thought Henry's religious reforms gave too much favor to the Huguenots. Unfortunately for the cause of religious toleration in France, Henry's reforms were overturned by his grandson Louis XIV, who in 1685 revoked the Edict of Nantes and proclaimed Roman Catholicism as the established religion of France. Louis made this move to gain the pope's favor and the right to use the title Most Christian King. Again, decisions were made based on politics and power, not religion; again the cause of religion was used as justification to hold onto power.

Across Europe, fears that the revocation of the Edict of Nantes could reignite the violence of the religious wars were not realized. Instead what resulted was an exodus of thousands of French Huguenots who chose to leave their homeland to settle in countries that practiced religious toleration: Holland, England, Switzerland. The Prussian Elector of Brandenburg in northern Germany, Frederick Wilhelm I, invited an assembly of Huguenots who had escaped France for Holland to settle in Potsdam, knowing their skills and industry could be useful for Prussia's economy. If you visit the Old Town in Potsdam today, you will see quaint red brick shops and warehouses built in the seventeenth-century Dutch architectural style, the legacy of the Huguenots. Another group of Huguenots, who had settled in the German Palatinate, called Pfalz, eventually immigrated to New York colony in 1678 and built a town in the Hudson Valley called New Paltz, one of the earliest Huguenot villages in colonial America.

When I got back to the village after Sunday Mass in Goudargues, I wandered around the old fortress walls, gazing at the massive towers, and tried to imagine this peaceful place as it was in 1565 under Huguenot siege. According to the history detailed at the *Maison de Patrimonie et Histoire,* our village had remained Catholic and loyal to the Monarchy during the Wars of Religion, which made it a target for the Huguenots. I could picture Montmorency's Huguenot army firing cannonballs against the walls, the flaming missiles hurled by the medieval mangonels that set the town ablaze, and the terrified people desperately trying to save their lives and property. It was heartbreaking to imagine, yet sobering to think that if I had been living here in 1565, attending Mass would be very dangerous.

∽ ∾

Believing that the religious conflicts were long over, I was surprised to learn from my history books that France did not "disestablish"—that is, did not officially separate the church from the state until 1905. The driving factor in that reform was the Dreyfus Affair of 1890, when a French-Jewish captain in the army was accused and convicted of treason because he was Jewish. The crisis was so controversial and so polarizing for the French secular society—there were bands of "Dreyfusards" and "anti-Dreyfusards"—that the left-wing cabinet of the Third Republic was able to enact a new law to separate religion from government, which, among other reforms, transferred church property to state ownership. The law states, "The Republic neither recognizes, nor salaries, nor subsidizes any religion." In effect, the state took control of the buildings of the four sects—Roman Catholic, Calvinist Protestant, Lutheran Protestant, and Jewish—maintaining them at public expense. However, the operation of the religious organizations was no longer controlled by the state. Most important, the state no longer controlled the selection of the bishops, relinquishing the right that had been claimed by the Constituent Assembly during the French Revolution.

As far back as the Middle Ages, the bishops were wealthy land-owners and held secular as well as religious power. Perhaps because of the tremendous wealth and power the state derived from con-trolling the church, France was late in formal disestablishment. This from the nation that was a leader of the eighteenth-century Age of Enlightenment inspired by philosophers such as the Frenchmen Voltaire and Diderot, the Swiss Rousseau, and the Englishman John Locke, who upheld the principles of intellectual freedom per-sonal autonomy, scientific progress, and religious toleration. The Enlightenment influenced Thomas Jefferson and James Madison to include Locke's ideas from *Letters Concerning Toleration*, which outlined the principle of the separation of church and state, in the United States Constitution. The actual wording of the First Amendment states, "Congress shall make no law respecting the establishment of a religion, or prohibiting the exercise of same." The phrase "separa-tion of church and state" is found in a letter from Jefferson to a Baptist congregation in 1802 and has since entered the language of America's political discourse. Still, the frequency with which the issue of separation of church and state surfaces in our national news indicates how difficult, perhaps impossible, that separation is. It is not a firewall.

The most important historical event in France that was the beginning of the end of the church-state symbiosis, and arguably the pivotal event in modern history, was the French Revolution. It is such a massive subject that any attempt to discuss it in less than 300,000 words will fall prey to the charge of oversimplifi-cation. Historians are continually refining their analyses of the causes and effects of the French Revolution and the extent of the political, social, philosophical, and psychological ramifications in the years following. But what is generally agreed is that the French Revolution changed European life forever. What may not be as well-known is how the French Revolution was the first step in what ultimately resulted in the constitutional separation of the church from the French state. Whether this revolutionary call for church reform stemmed from the Enlightenment or from what French radicals observed from the American Revolution is not clear. We do know that the abuses of absolute power resulted in the complete abandonment of the *Ancien Régime* and its hand-in-glove relationship with the church and the clergy. Incidentally, the financial crisis of 1787–1788 that forced King Louis XVI to call the Estates General was in a large part due to France's military support of the American colonists in their struggle for independence from Great Britain. French motives were not entirely sympathetic, however. France had come out on the losing end after the Seven Years War (the French and Indian War was the North American theatre of the European conflict), and the French wanted to help anyone who had the British as a common enemy. I remember an old Arabic saying: "The enemy of my enemy is my friend."

Dating back to the fourteenth century, the three Estates of the *Ancien Régime* were made up of the clergy—the First Estate—and the nobility—the Second Estate. These two groups were tightly bound and mutually dependent. The power of the church was well entrenched; for example, the state taxes levied on the people included a church tithe. The church was the largest landowner in France and was enriched from the feudal wealth that was derived from it. By the eighteenth century, the upper clergy—the bishops and cardinals—were exclusively of the noble class.

The Third Estate was made up of everyone else—lawyers, bankers, bourgeoisie, laborers, and merchant tradesmen, who saw the power and wealth firmly in the control of the first two privileged orders. A famous pamphlet written by the Abbé Sieyès in 1789 carried the title *"Qu'est-ce que le Tiers Etat?"* ("What is the Third Estate?") and concluded that only the Third Estate truly made up the French nation. When the Third Estate declared itself to be the National Assembly in 1789 and established a Constitution in 1791, a complete elimination of the church's power in civil affairs began. Along with political upheavals, land reforms, and economic transition from feudalism to capitalism, the period of the Revolution saw a sweeping rejection of religion and the clergy. The reaction became an overreaction that resulted in the destruction of many works of religious art and architecture. In Paris the churches and abbeys were ransacked and vandalized, and religious statues and artworks were thrown into the Seine. The Constituent Assembly ordered the confiscation of all ecclesiastical property in 1789 and nationalized the church. In the excesses of the Reign of Terror, hundreds of priests and bishops were executed, along with aristocrats and monarchist bourgeois. The Committee of Public Safety headed by Robespierre abolished the use of the Gregorian calendar and created a Cult of the Supreme Being in an effort to turn the populace away from the traditional church. When Napoleon Bonaparte seized power in the *coup d'etat* of 18 Brumaire Year VIII, using the Revolutionary calendar, or what was 9 November 1799 to the rest of Europe, he reintroduced the traditional religious practices to legitimize his regime. The Concordat of 1801 between the new regime of Napoleon and the papacy in Rome restored some of the pre-Revolutionary rights of the church while initiating others, such as the government selection of the clergy. The Concordat reaffirmed the secular nature of the French state, and it remained in effect until 1905 when the law was passed to disestablish the Catholic Church in France. Now I will cease with my oversimplification.

Today the constitution of France contains the secular concept of *Laïcité*, defined as the respect of freedom of expression and freedom of religion. The term, which dates from the late 1800s, is related to the French word for laity, which is anything that is not clergy, and asserts that France is a secular republic. The modern, secular traditions of France are developed to the point that, unlike in the United States, the installation ceremony for the French president does not include an oath of office sworn on a Bible. However, the recent controversy of the new law banning the Muslim burka in public places serves to remind us that there are still unresolved issues with the implementation of separation of church and state. Should such symbols be treated as culture and religion or intolerance and fanaticism? Perhaps we need a New Enlightenment that could furnish us with updated philosophical guidelines to help chart a path between toleration and freedom of expression, while maintaining the preservation of cultural differences and ancient traditions. A delicate balance to maintain, indeed.

CHAPTER 10

The Franks

In what seems yet another example of serendipity, I had a chance to travel to southern France one late December after Christmas to attend to some construction work being done on the house below the château. My normal pattern had been to spend two or three weeks at the house during my summer vacations, so I had not yet seen the countryside in midwinter. Even though the trip was for only a short interval, and I had to meet with the contractor and some of the other workmen, I had a little time to experience Provence in late December and observe the seasonal changes. After the flight to France, I did the familiar drive from Lyon, noticing how the landscape had been modified by winter. The colors of the countryside were muted; little more than hazy earth tones, with bare tree branches silhouetted against a gray sky, and plowed fields. The smaller towns I passed through still had some Christmas decorations strung on lampposts, giving the impression of unhurried winter doldrums. Sundown came quite early, much before I reached the Cèze Valley, so, upon arrival I settled into the house in the darkness and waited patiently till the next day to explore.

With the morning light, I stepped out on the terrace and got my first good look at the village in winter. The fields of grapevines that stretched on both sides of the river and had been so green the previous summer were now a brownish gray, and the leafless trees by the bridge permitted me to see the full extent of the *Pont Charles Martel*. The river was covered in a misty blanket that wound around the hills in the south toward Sabran. The air was chilly and damp, and carried the smoky aroma of burning vine braches. After breakfast I decided to walk down to the *Cascades du Sautadet*. Bundled up against the *mistral*, the north wind, I stepped carefully over the damp stones and gravel of the zigzag path through town. No one was about—no tourists, hikers, or local inhabitants. When I passed the *mairie*, I heard water gurgling and noticed the *lavoir*, the communal washing tank, was full of water; it was the first time I had ever seen water in the stone tank. I wasn't sure what the source was, perhaps an underground spring that dried up in the summer. The sky seemed to be clearing, but the air still carried the hint of the log fires warming the houses, and the smoke from the chimneys hinted that the village wasn't entirely deserted. Gusts of the cold, *mistral* wind that cut through my wool coat gave explanation enough for why the locals would be indoors. But I persevered past the church and around the corner of the last house by the World War I memorial. I came upon the field of grapevines closest to the edge of town. This field is featured in every summer photograph of the village, resplendent in shiny, lush green leaves on vines planted in neat rows, soaking up the sunlight. Now in midwinter, the bare vines had been pruned down to their basics, all brown and gnarled in straight rows; they resembled small, sturdy stick-figure soldiers in formation, arms outstretched and flexing their biceps.

When I reached the waterfalls, the level of the river was very high, and the water was crashing through the limestone channels of the Cascade, stronger than I had ever seen it. The dried white mud on the stones and the dead leaves and twigs in the bushes on the banks indicated that the river had been above flood level recently. A few other intrepid hikers were out, and if they were like me, they were thinking about getting back inside and warming their cold toes by the fire. But I had to admit, the countryside was beautiful in winter, even without all the leafy finery. There was something nobly elemental in the look of the bare trees that edged the fields, the rows of gnarled grapevines, and the mists that hung around the river.

That evening, curled up under a blanket on the sofa with a glass of wine, I again started to wonder: What is it about Provence? In a larger sense, what is it about France? What is it that fascinates, that confounds, that mesmerizes, that frustrates? Why is it that when we see something, be it fashion, interior design, architecture, or artwork, whether we taste the food or hear the music, we know it is French? What is it about this country with its influences from the Celts, the Greeks, the Romans, and the Goths? How is it that France became so dominant in European history that the French language was from the 1700s to the mid-twentieth century the *lingua franca*, the language of diplomacy, of culture and enlightenment? What *is* it about France?

Indeed, a question, a huge question, impossible to answer, but interesting to consider on a long winter night. I can't help thinking that if the Romans had never been the powerhouse of the Western world and Gaul had not been overrun by Roman Legions, France today would be completely different. But the other factor—as important, I believe—was the Germanic invasions of the third century, and not just any Germanic tribe, but the Franks, that amorphous, mysterious group of people made up of a hodgepodge of older tribes who reconstituted themselves to become the Franks.

Frankish kings, Cluny Museum, Paris

So who were the Franks? Their origins are steeped in myth and legend, and historians cannot even agree on the meaning of their name. Many years ago a colleague of mine who was aware of my interest in history encouraged me to read history from primary sources, those writers who were closest in time and location to the events they were documenting. That is how I first read *The History of the Franks* by the sixth-century historian Gregory, Bishop of Tours. Gregory states that the original land of the Franks was Pannonia, the ancient name of what is now Slovenia and Hungary, and briefly describes the Franks' migration to the Rhine in the third century. The other important contemporary source is the *Chronicle of Fredegar*, a late sixth-century history of the Franks. The monk Fredegar (584–641) gives a more fanciful genealogy of the Franks as stretching back to ancient kings of Troy, and tells us that the Franks were named for their early king, called Francio, who led them out of the East to settle on the banks of the Rhine. This story is so similar to the story of the founding of Rome in the *Aeneid* by Virgil, where the Trojan prince Aeneas escaped the burning of Troy and settled in Italy, leaving the foundation of Rome to his grandson Romulus, it must be intentional. I suppose this epic association with ancient Troy enhances the prestige and *gravitas* of the Frankish Kingdom, just as Virgil was attempting to do for Rome in the *Aeneid* and the connection with Homer and his Greek epics, the *Iliad* and *Odyssey*. I prefer another possible meaning of the name Franks, from the Medieval Latin *francus*, meaning free, which, if true, indicates how the Franks regarded themselves—as the Free People.

Current historians agree that the Franks arose as an identifiable people in the first century AD, but as a loose confederation of older Germanic tribes, the Chattuarii, the Amsivarii, the Bructeri, and the Salii that had migrated from their prehistoric homelands in the upper Rhine Valley to the mouth of the Rhine. How these tribes were related, if at all, and how and why they came to form a confederacy is a mystery. Historians use the term *ethnogenesis* to describe the process of tribal breakdown and recombination, such as what produced the Franks. When the Roman historians Pliny and Tacitus, writing in first century AD, described the Germanic tribes in general, the Franks were occupying the land roughly covering what is now northwest Germany, Belgium, and the Netherlands.

In the fourth century AD, the Franks were part of the Great Migration of Germanic tribes, the westward crossing of the Rhine River, the Roman frontier of Gaul, and occupying territory that had been Roman for five hundred years. When I was a kid in school, this sequence of events was taught to us as the Fall of the Roman Empire and the beginning of the Dark Ages. However, this view has been softened recently to a less melodramatic one and is now regarded as "the transformation of the World of Late Antiquity." According to twentieth-century scholars, such as J. Wallace-Hadrill and Peter Brown, Rome didn't suddenly fall but rather underwent a gradual transformation starting in the second century and continuing to the early seventh century. The shift was so gradual that the Gallo-Romans living in southern France may not have noticed any changes in their daily lives. Instead of the seventeenth-century view as presented in Edward Gibbon's monumental work, *The Decline and Fall of the Roman Empire*, we can consider a more tempered perspective of the fate of the Roman Empire—that of transformation, not extinction. I have trained myself not to think in terms of the Dark Ages, but instead the World of Late Antiquity.

∞ ∞

The empire that started with Augustus from the power struggle after Julius Caesar's assassination was a political triumph. Augustus ushered in a period of relative peace and stability, the *Pax Romana* that permitted prosperity, growth, commerce, trade, and the rise of a merchant class. This *Pax Romana* continued until the empire's Eastern frontiers were attacked by the Parthians in late 161 AD. To respond to the threat, Roman Emperor Marcus Aurelius, who reigned from 161 to 180, moved three Legions from the Rhône and Danube eastward for defense. A group of restive barbarians, called the Marcomanni, saw this weakening of the Danube frontier as their chance to challenge Rome and, in 166 AD, crossed the Danube to ravage the rich Roman provinces. They moved through Pannonia, skirting the Adriatic, and reached northern Italy conducting raids near modern Venice. The safety of the empire frontier had been breached, the empire was exposed as vulnerable to attack, and the "time of troubles" for Rome had begun.

After a period of relative stability following the Marcomannic Wars, the empire frontiers were again under pressure from the barbarians across the Rhine and Danube from around 235 to 284 AD, referred to by historians as the Crisis of the Third Century. Theories abound as to why the empire frontier came under attack by the barbarians in the third century. The undisputed reaction by Rome resulted in reform—military, administrative, and importantly, cultural reform. The Emperor Diocletian's administrative and economic reforms; the Emperor Constantine's acceptance of Christianity and the establishment of the eastern empire capital of Constantinople; the treaty of Theodosius with the Goths after the defeat and death of Emperor Valens at Adrianopolis in 378 AD, which allowed the Goths to settle within the Empire, were all steps in the direction of transformation. The Roman Empire, which at its largest in 117 AD stretched from northwest Africa to Persia and Egypt to Britain, was just too large to be governed centrally from the city of Rome. Diocletian split the empire into a western empire administered from Rome and an eastern empire administered from Constantinople. The increased pressures from the barbarians on the overstretched, extensive frontiers required drastic solutions to regain stability and peace.

The consequence of these solutions brought reform to the military along the Danube and Rhine frontier, and made the military a civilizing influence, Gallo-Roman civilization. The Roman Legions that protected the frontiers had been for years, even generations, stationed at the same locations; the soldiers themselves were native to the frontier lands. These soldiers were in closest contact with the barbarian German tribes at the edges of the empire and were instrumental in conveying Roman culture in the forms of commercial transaction. The Legion soldiers purchased grain and fresh meat from the barbarian merchants. Trade contact developed in the other direction also, and Roman merchants introduced the extravagance of wealth to the barbarians. In time the barbarians couldn't do without the luxury goods they traded for with the Romans. Archaeological discoveries along the western frontier indicate a brisk trade from the first to the third centuries; jewelry, coins, and weapons manufactured in the East show up from time to time in frontier regions of northern Europe. The Free People of Germany had "come under the spell of Rome," as stated by Professor Geary. One important policy of Roman government was the acceptance of the barbarian people of the conquered lands as Roman citizens, a policy called Romanization, which strengthened the Roman populace by introducing new strains of vigorous people willing to be assimilated and coexist in peace. Thus the distinctions between Roman and barbarian blurred—a process that has been described by Professor Geary as the Romanization of the Barbarian and the Barbarization of the Roman.

The barbarian Franks held a genuine respect and admiration for the Roman past. They used the cultural and spiritual values of classical antiquity to define what gives life meaning. From the Roman perspective, it was advantageous to extend their influence over the Franks as well as other barbarians in order to open markets for Roman luxury goods. The cultivation of commercial trading partners defused frontier tensions. As in our modern world, mutually beneficial trading partners tend to avoid war. Rome's goal of making the barbarians dependent on trade with the Legions created the frontier stability Rome desired. However, the introduction of luxury goods to barbarian society had a destabilizing effect among the barbarians, creating an economic hierarchy in the population that led to pro-Roman factions made up of the wealthy aristocrats and anti-Roman factions made up of laborers.

Who were these Germanic tribes, these barbarians? Attempts to subdivide them into groups usually name the East Germanic people—Goths, Burgundians, and Vandals—and the West Germanic people—the Saxons, Bavarians, Alemanni, and the Franks. Anthropologists have identified these Germanic tribes with the Iron Age people who created the Jastorf Culture, the people whom Julius Caesar called Germans, though the Greek historians made only passing reference to the group. The people of the Jastorf Culture occupied the northern parts of central Europe and southern areas of Scandinavia from around the sixth century BC and are contemporary with the Celtic Hallstatt and La Tène cultures in what is now Switzerland and Austria. These barbarians were not the knuckle-dragging troglodytes as satirized in comedy skits or TV commercials. They were enterprising, energetic people who desired prosperity and security, and who appreciated the ancient Greco-Roman culture and civilization. These are the people who built the foundation of Western civilization, the ancestors of Europeans and a good number of Americans.

The German tribes with the greatest effect on the history of Provence include the Goths, the Burgundians, and the Franks. References to Goths and the Gothic survive today in lurid horror-romance novels and the ghastly fashions of a youth subculture, and it seems as though the original meaning of Gothic has been forgotten, which is a pity. The story of the real Goths somewhat parallels the Franks in terms of ethnogenesis. It has been suggested that the island of Gotland in southern Sweden may be one homeland of the Goths. As part of the inexplicable migrations of the third century, the Goths started moving east and south as loosely organized bands, occupying large areas stretching from the northern shore of the Black Sea west to the Roman province of Dacia, modern Romania. The Goths took advantage of the weakening of the Roman frontiers, and one group invaded eastern parts of the empire, including Turkey and the Balkan Peninsula, but were subdued enough to reach a truce with Rome to confine themselves to Dacia. These Goths became known as the Tervingi, and later, as the Visigoths, they invaded Provence and settled in Spain, creating the Visigothic Kingdom with the capital at Toulouse in southern France. Another Gothic people, called Greutungi, continued to live along the north coast of the Black Sea until the arrival of the Huns in 376 AD forced the Greutungi to join the Hunnic confederation. The death of Attila the Hun in 453 led to the collapse of the Hunnic forces, allowing the Greutungi to re-emerge as the Ostrogoths. Thus the two main Gothic confederations appear in history, and both were destined to have a significant influence on the course of Western civilization.

While the Ostrogoths more or less confined themselves to the Italian peninsula and the Visigoths were strongest in Provence and Spain, the northern lands of what is now Belgium and the Netherlands fell under the control of the Franks. One group of Franks emerged as dominant, the Salii or Salians. Their tribal leaders affected the barbarian fashion of the day of growing their hair long as a mark of chiefdom, leading to later references as the Long-Haired Kings, or *Reges criniti*. The tribe of Salians produced the military leaders of the Franks, who, through warfare with neighboring Germanic tribes and alliances with the Gallo-Roman leaders, gained a position of dominance in the mid-fifth century. In these early years, the Salian Franks learned the surest way to wealth and prestige was through alliance with Rome.

Gregory of Tours describes the earliest of these Frankish Long-Haired Kings as the shadowy Chlodio, whose son Merovech gave the name to the Merovingian Dynasty. Merovech's son Childeric (died c. 481) was the first historically authenticated Frankish chieftain; his grave near Tournai, Belgium, was discovered in 1653, containing numerous rich grave goods attesting to his kingship. Childeric was wise enough to forge alliances with the Gallo Romans of Gaul and be seen as a protector of *Romanitas*, the Roman way of life and society. His actions set the stage for his son Clovis to take over as leader of the Salian Franks in 482. Because it was almost expected for military leaders to expand the lands under their command, Clovis set about attacking the neighboring regions to create a Frankish hegemony. The kingdom of Soissons, which was centered around Paris, the land of the Thuringi on the west bank of the Rhine, and the territory of the Alemanni around Trier all fell under Clovis's control. The Battle of Tolbiac in 497, the great victory of Clovis's Franks against the Alemanni, was one of the most important battles in the history of France; the outcome influenced the future of French culture, religion, and language.

Clovis is considered by many to be the founder of the first royal dynasty in France's history. His name has appeared in medieval texts as Chlodovic, Chlodivicus, and Chlodowech; these names have evolved into the modern Ludwig, Luigi, Louis, and Lewis, but he is best known as Clovis. Because of his victories over the last Barbarian Roman general, Syragius of Soissons; the Alemanni; and the Arian Visigoths; Clovis united most of Gaul, comprised of Neustria, Austrasia, and Burgundy, under the control of the Salian Franks. His name still appears in modern business and advertisements; I remember seeing a large freight-hauling truck on the highway to Marseille with the name "Clovis" emblazoned on the side. Clovis's long-haired descendants, the Merovingians, stayed in power for the next two centuries; most of their history was described by Gregory of Tours in blood-curdling detail, but only up to the death of King Childerbert II in 591, just before Gregory's death in 594. By the late seventh century, the Merovingians' grasp on the kingship had deteriorated to the point that later chroniclers such as Fredegar refer to them as *rois fainéants*, do-nothing kings. The real power was being consolidated into the office of *maior domus*, mayor of the palace, a sort of chancellor serving the do-nothing kings who had become regal window-dressing. In 686, Pepin II of Herstal became duke of Austrasia and, in 688, began to gain control of Neustria and Burgundy, completing consolidation of the Frankish kingdom. He ruled without a Merovingian king, which gives us some idea of how powerful he had become. When he died in 714, he divided his kingdom in the Frankish fashion among his three sons. His illegitimate son, Charles Martel, "the Hammer," rose in power and won a famous victory over invading Saracens in 732 near Poitiers, arguably one of the most important battles in Western history. The dynasty called Carolingian is named for him.

The Franks' area of influence had been mainly the land north of the Loire, with evidence of only a few excursions into Provence. However, with the encroaching Muslim Moors, who had overrun Spain and crossed the Pyrenees, Charles Martel gave much more attention to defending the south. His exploits in Provence between 720 and 730 were at the behest of one of the local princes, Abbo, who was vying for power against another prince, Maurontus. While Maurontus appealed to the Moors besieging northern Spain and Narbonne for support, Abbo went with Charles Martel—yet another example of being careful with whom you form an alliance. Charles conducted a series of expeditions in the southern Rhône

Valley, seeing this as an opportunity to become the champion of Christianity against Moorish incursions and thereby earn the favor of the papacy. Charles Martel succeeded in expelling the Moors from the Rhône Valley, but not without great destruction to cities such as Avignon, and the control of Provence ultimately fell to the Carolingians. I find it easy to believe the bridge near the village was named for him to commemorate his heroism against the Moors.

One of Charles Martel's sons (and my favorite name in French history) was *Pépin le Bref*, Pepin the Short, who became *maior domus*, mayor of the palace, for Childeric III and managed to depose this last of Clovis's descendants in a coup in 751 with the approval of Pope Zachary. The deal included Pepin capturing the Papal States in Italy from the Ostrogoths and restoring them to the papacy, called the Donation of Pepin. In gratitude the pope conferred the title Protector of the Romans on Pepin and his descendants. His most illustrious descendant was his son Charles the Great, Charlemagne.

Charlemagne remains one of the most famous figures of the Middle Ages. Separating the legends and romances from the historical man can be difficult for some heroes, such as Frederick Barbarossa, and impossible for others, such as King Arthur. Fortunately we have two chronicles of the life of Charlemagne: the first by a contemporary, Einhard, who wrote the *Vita Caroli*, and the second being the chronicle *De Carlo Magno* by a man known as the Monk of St. Gall, written some seventy years after Charlemagne's death.

Born in 741 or 742 depending on the source, Charles was the elder son of Pepin the Short, though illegitimate, and he inherited Pepin's ambition, energy, and ruthlessness. After Pepin's death in 768, the Frankish kingdom was divided between Charles and Pepin's younger son, Carloman. When Carloman unexpectedly but conveniently died in 771, Charles acted quickly to exile Carloman's widow and disinherit his two sons, reuniting the kingdom of Pepin the Short. Neither Einhard nor the Monk of St. Gall chastised

Charles in print for this gross injustice, perhaps because they were beneficiaries of the patronage and wealth of the Frankish Kingdom under the Carolingians. For the next forty-three years, Charles, through warfare and/or diplomacy, increased the lands of the Frankish kingdom to include what is today most of Germany, Austria, Holland, Belgium, Switzerland, northern Italy, and France excluding Brittany. He accomplished this by conquering the Saxons in Germany and deposing the Langobard king in Italy and claiming the title of King of the Langobards while renewing the Donation of Pepin with the papacy. His campaign across the Pyrenees into Visigothic Spain, however, was a military failure, and the retreat of his army through the Roncesvelles Pass was the scene of a disaster. The Basques ambushed and destroyed the rearguard commanded by Roland, an event immortalized in the eleventh-century *Chanson de Roland* and retold and embellished over the centuries.

Perhaps Charlemagne's most important legacy for the history of Western civilization is what is now called the Carolingian Renaissance, ushered in because of his interest in scholarship and his devotion to the Roman Church. He invited noted scholars such as the Englishman Alcuin of York; Paul the Deacon, a Langobard historian; and Einhard, who was later his biographer; to join his administration with the goal of advancing higher learning in the Frankish realm. Alcuin organized the Palace School at Aachen, Charlemagne's capital, for the education of any talented youth, rich or poor. Monastic schools were also founded, and monks in the scriptoria began copying ancient Roman, Greek, or Arabic texts, developing an improved standardized script that increased legibility and comprehension across the kingdom and saved a wealth of ancient literature that might have been lost. (In my younger, artistic days, I dabbled in calligraphy and I found the Carolingian script to be lovely, functional and relatively easy to write.) Charlemagne also devoted much effort to codifying and enforcing the legal system based on tribal laws, setting up a judicial court, and introducing a jury system. The medieval feudal system, based on loyalty, honor, and service to the *seigneur*, that personal bond between king and office-holder, became entrenched, and with it developed the origins of the French nobility, the dukes and counts who controlled the fiefs that became territorial states within the kingdom. What we now think of as the days of chivalry, "when knighthood was in flower," was the result of the Carolingian Renaissance.

On Christmas Day in the year 800, Charlemagne was crowned Emperor of the Romans by Pope Leo III at old St. Peter's Basilica in Rome. One reason for this move was to formalize Frankish protection of the Latin papal states from the Greek Byzantine Empire in the east, which at that time was headed by—gasp—a woman, the Empress Irene; it also symbolically created what later became the Holy Roman Empire in the west. Frankish domination in Europe continued for the next three centuries, supporting the papacy while Frankish clergy spread the teachings of the Roman Catholic Church, as separate from the Greek Orthodox Church, and leading the Crusades to the Holy Land then establishing the Frankish Kingdom of Jerusalem. Their numbers in the Crusader armies were so disproportionately high that for many years Arabic Muslims labeled all Christian Europeans they met "Franks."

The name Frank survives in Franconia, now part of Bavaria in Germany, a remnant of the Holy Roman Empire. The empire itself survived until 1806 when Napoleon forced the Habsburg Emperor Francis II to abolish it. The Gothic architecture of the great cathedrals originated with the Franks. The currency introduced by Charlemagne, called the *livre carolienne* from the Latin *libre*, the Roman scale for weighing coins, became known as a *franc* in 1360 because it carried the minted inscription *Francorum Rex*, King of the Franks. The term *lingua franca*, Italian for Frankish tongue, has come to mean any language that serves as a medium of communication between nations. Words in our daily conversation, such as franchise and frankly, are derived from the Franks. Because of their energy, industry, and their claim to the Roman inheritance, the Franks have certainly left their imprint on the development and shaping of modern Europe.

The Salian Franks produced a set of law codes, the *Lex Salica*, which dates from the time of Clovis and is probably based on Gallic Roman Law and possibly influenced by Visigothic Law. Salian Law was mostly concerned with fines and penalties for murder and theft, settling land disputes, and generally avoiding blood feuds to preserve the peace. In the event of a murder, the law assigned payments from the perpetrator's family to the victim's family as compensation to avoid revenge killing. The payments were called *wergeld*, using a Germanic-Frankish word instead of Latin, and the law set the values of each member of society—robust men, child-bearing women, slaves, the elderly, and infants. Probably the most famous code in the *Lex* concerns inheritance, which states that women must be excluded from inheriting Salic land. This code has been invoked over the years to bar the women in royal families from claiming the throne in countries still observing the Salic Law. Famous examples of the application of Salic Law include the disinheriting of Edward III in 1328 that set off the 100 Years War between England and France; the heirless death of the Habsburg Emperor of Spain Charles II that in 1701 started the War of Spanish Succession; and the need for the Pragmatic Sanction of 1713 to override the Salic Law and allow the Habsburg Archduchess Maria Theresa to rule the Holy Roman Empire in 1740. Even today, the Queen of England may be closest in bloodline to claim the crown of Luxembourg or Belgium, but those countries cling to the Salic Law, which forbids female rule. Misogyny of the Middle Ages.

And that's another thing—the Frankish Kings. How did the concept of kingship emerge from the transformation of the Roman Empire? What was the origin of the nobility? How is it related to royalty? The *Lex Salica* doesn't contain provisions granting special privileges to a noble class, giving the impression that the Franks had no legal definition of nobility. But wealth, land, status, and political power defined the aristocracy then, as now, and the Frankish aristocracy, based on the old Gallo-Roman senatorial families of inherited wealth, developed along with the mythical concept of Merovingian royalty and royal blood. The idea of royal blood evolved into a hereditary monarchy and a belief in the divine right of kings, which the Bourbon King Louis XIV carried to the extreme. The concept of kingship is quite exotic, even fascinating to Americans, and the fact that we create our own royalty out of politicians, movie stars, and sports heroes suggests a subconscious need for royalty. Oh well, the Founding Fathers took care to protect us from that.

Even before the Carolingians, the Merovingians imposed the mystique of royal blood on the downtrodden Frankish peasants. If they had given the matter some thought, the peasants would have realized that royal blood lines could be traced back to European Stone Age men, just like peasant blood lines. But the mystique of the *Sang Royal* had a good run. The gifts and qualities a particular family had to have to merit the designator of "royal" remains a mystery to me. But certain families rose above the others to produce the line of French kings, from the Merovingians and the Carolingians to the Robertians to the Capetians to the Valois to the Bourbons. That covers about fourteen hundred years of kingship and ended only with the Revolutions of 1789 and 1848. It is fascinating to think the current king of Spain is descended from a long line of Bourbons and can trace his ancestry back to thirteenth-century France.

❧ ❧

About halfway through my winter sojourn in the village, Marc and Kate joined me. They had driven down from Berlin where they were on business. We had a clever plan to spend New Year's Eve together in Paris. Rather than drive we took the high-speed TGV, *le Train de Grande Vitesse*, from Avignon to the *Gare de Lyon* in Paris, covering the 580 km (360 miles) in about 2.5 hours, giving us the whole afternoon of New Year's Eve to wander around the city devoid of tourists. We quickly discovered Paris was full of partying Parisians. We were unable to get a table for lunch at Les Truffes Folies, one of Marc and Kate's favorite bistros, but easily found a second choice. The weather was cold, damp, and rain threatened, so after some shopping, we started back to our hotel to rest and clean up for dinner that evening at the elegant restaurant La Fontaine Gaillon where Marc had made reservations. Walking past the Tuilleries Gardens on our way back to our hotel, we made a detour to peek into the elegant lobby of Hotel Meurice, one of the scenes from the World War II book and movie *Is Paris Burning?* In August 1944, during the last days before Paris was liberated, the German *Wehrmacht* commandant had his headquarters at the Hotel Meruice, and he was under orders from Hitler to destroy Paris, orders that he thankfully ignored.

Marc wanted me to see the Place des Vosges, his favorite square in Paris, so we made another detour which was a bit of a walk. But it was worth it: the lovely seventeenth century square with an equestrian statue of King Louis XIII was filled with families and couples enjoying the winter afternoon, and the shops underneath the stone and brick arcades surrounding the square were charming. After another long trek back to the Arc de Triomphe and stopping for a cognac against the cold at the Café Winston, we decided we were tired of walking and finally caught a cab for our hotel to dress for dinner.

We were the first diners to arrive at the posh restaurant, La Fontaine Gaillon, so we had all the attention of the wait staff. When some fellow revelers were seated at the adjacent table, we struck up a conversation with them, finding out they were Danish businessmen and their wives. The dinner was fantastic, and the wine flowed. As midnight approached, the waiters brought out glasses of champagne and small marzipan cakes for everyone. One older gentleman at a nearby table counted down the seconds, and at the stroke of midnight, the lights in the dining room were dimmed, and we all cheered and clinked glasses in the candlelight. I was just tipsy enough to ask the Danish man at the next table to sing "Auld Lang Syne" with me—probably not a tradition in Denmark—and he did his best. When we were done with our rendition, the other patrons applauded and raised their champagne glasses to us! Dinner and a show. After fortifying ourselves with glasses of cognac and exchanging good-byes with our dinner companions, we rose to leave. All of the diners turned to us and again raised their glasses with smiles and called out, *"Bonne Année!"* and "Happy New Year!" which I was only too happy to return. How often can one claim to be a hit among sophisticated and well-heeled Parisians?

We walked somewhat unsteadily back to our hotel with the gorgeous Paris Opera house in the distance flood-lit against the night sky. The streets were filled with revelers, and car horns honked as we crossed the huge courtyard in front of the *Louvre* with the glass pyramid on one side and the small *Arc de Triumph du Carrousel* on the other. The Eiffel Tower was fantastically lit for New Year's, and all the magnificent buildings, monuments, and bridges seemed to glow in the dark. What a city! *When I get home,* I thought, *I should watch the movie* Is Paris Burning? *and bless the memory of the German commandant who disobeyed Hitler and refused to destroy Paris.* Once we crossed the *Pont du Carousel* and entered the smaller streets of Saint-Germain-des-Prés, we became thoroughly disoriented and had to hail a cab. When we tumbled into the back and gave the address to the cabdriver, he said laconically, *"Pas loin"* (not far), and indeed we were only a block away. Whew, that cognac!

I met Marc and Kate for breakfast at the Café Les Deux Magots—a favorite café of early twentieth-century Parisian intelligentsia such as Jean-Paul Sartre, Simone de Beauvoir, Earnest Hemingway, Pablo Picasso, and Albert Camus. For me, dashing down fashionable Parisian boulevards seemed a romantic dream come true. However, whenever I'm in Paris I always regret that I don't look like Audrey Hepburn or Grace Kelly. I was allowed in the café anyway. After breakfast we caught a cab for the *Gare de Lyon* and returned to Avignon on the TGV. After another day with me in the village, Marc and Kate packed up their car and left for Berlin. My winter dreams were coming to a close.

In my time remaining, I thought over the great fun we had in Paris and considered how different that Paris visit had been from my first experience. I thought of the people we met and the many kind, friendly faces. Not the typical stereotype one would expect. After this experience I don't see how there could be a French stereotype. Indeed, the French people seem to be made up of an endless variety. I wondered again: what is it about the French? I recalled how the French people today started out in the first century BC with a foundation of the Celts and Gallo-Romans, layered with the Franks and Visigoths. This mixture created the cultural substrate that observed the subsequent introduction of people from such places as North Africa, Indochina, and the Middle East. The introduction of non-Europeans is the legacy of the years of French colonialism and imperialism and evidence of the fact France sits on the crossroads of western trade and commerce. Complicating the matter further, the modern French state is made up of what had been separate regions, each with their own culture, dialect, and customs, which is very much in evidence today. How can one nation be built on such a foundation? I remembered the famous statement of Charles de Gaulle: "How can anyone govern a nation that has 246 different kinds of cheese?" According to current social philosophers, French culture has no ethnic basis; rather, the acceptance of

French culture and language determines one to be French, not race or ethnic origin. I believe this explains the high degree of importance the French place on their language and culture. Contemporary writers claim that there is no such thing as ethnic French and that French people are made up of the multiple ethnic tribes that have overrun France since the Neolithic times, which seems to be true. In his 1882 essay, "What is a Nation?" the French philosopher Earnest Renan defined a nation as a group of people willing to live together, which sidesteps the whole ethnic question.

How do the French regard themselves, their past, their history? Today's French people may not want to admit being the descendants of the Franks, but instead prefer to focus on the Gallo-Romans and then skip to the time of Charlemagne, followed by the monarchy and then to the republic. Given the chronicles of Merovingian history, that reluctance may be understandable. Reading in Gregory of Tours about Merovingian murder and mayhem, the brutality, and the treachery of the Frankish royal family is quite disturbing. One character stands out for sheer evil—Queen Fredegunde, the wife of Chilperic and the most horrid woman I have ever read about. I have entertained the notion that she was the model for every wicked stepmother stereotype for the Brothers Grimm and the Disney animated films. Eventually the Merovingians exhausted themselves to become the *rois faineant*, the do-nothing kings, and were quietly put away. They were guilty of wickedness in their early years and incompetence in their later years, and faded from history, lingering as figures of ridicule. The French nursery song *"Le Bon Roi Dagobert"* the Good King Dagobert, is anything but flattering. Who wouldn't want to disavow any relation to those people? But history is inescapable, a succession of events and factors that contribute to the present state. It is useless to try to alter history to suit a perceived legacy. And the Franks are part of the French legacy. If ever a country had a national legacy, it is France.

It is disappointing to realize I'm no closer to defining what is it about the French, except to recognize the history stretching back 2,500 years: the ethnic and cultural contributions of the Gallo-Romans and the Franks and the Goths, who were themselves ethnically and culturally heterogeneous; the Roman Church's influence on art and architecture; the effect of the land and climate on agriculture and industry; and the imprint of years of war, plague, and famine on the national psyche. The chemistry of shared memory and the catalysts of climate and environment continue to produce the unique French culture that inspires me every time I come here. Drowsily immersed in my ruminations, I realized it is way past bedtime.

Two days after Marc and Kate left, I was scheduled to leave. The short, misty days of winter in the Valley of the Cèze were ending for me. I could feel myself shutting down already—no more excursions, no more train rides, no more grocery trips, no more souvenir shopping. I would do all the cleaning and organizing needed to close and lock up the house. I counted backward from my flight time so I knew how early I had to be on the road to St. Exupéry airport in Lyon.

In the dim light of the last morning, I schlepped my luggage to the car and then locked the massive front door shutters. How many times have I left from this house to return to reality, taking away photos, books, bottles of wine, packages of lavender soap, and happy memories? I know I'll return, but still I must linger to gaze about me. I can feel already how much I'll miss my adventures here, how I'll treasure the time spent. *Don't worry,* I tell myself. Take that last, long look over your shoulder—you will come back. There is still so much to learn.

List of Maps and Photographs

Page 158: Frankish kings, Cluny Museum, Paris
Back cover: Author photo

See antiquitiesresearchllc.com for full-color photographs

Selected Bibliography

Works cited or consulted:

Bainton, Roland H. *Here I Stand—A Life of Martin Luther*. London: Penguin Books, 1950.

Brown, Peter. *The World of Late Antiquity*. New York: W.W. Norton and Company, 1989.

Bury, J. B. *History of the Later Roman Empire, Vol 1*. New York: The Encyclopedia Press, 1907, 1913.

Cassius Dio. *Roman History*. Translated by Earnest Cary. Loeb Classical Library. Harvard: Harvard University Press, 1917.

Clark, Kenneth. *Civilisation*. New York: Harper and Row, 1969.

Cunliffe, Barry. *Rome and Her Empire*. New York: McGraw-Hill, 1978.

Devic, Claude et Vaissete, Joseph, Benedictines de la Congregation de Saint-Maur. *Histoire Generale de LANGUEDOC, avec des notes et les pieces justifications.* Toulouse: Edouard Privat, Libraire — Editeur. Tome Premier, MDCCCLXXII.

Einhard and Notker the Stammerer. *Two Lives of Charlemagne.* Translated by Lewis Thorpe. New York: Penguin Classics, 1969.

Fletcher, Richard. *The Barbarian Conversion.* New York: Henry Holt, 1997.

Fredegar. *The Fourth Book of the Chronicle of Fredegar.* Translated by J.M. Wallace-Hadrill. London: Thomas Nelson and Sons, Ltd., 1960.

Frieda, Leonie. *Catherine de Medici—Renaissance Queen of France.* New York: Harper Perennial, 2006.

Geary, Patrick J. *Before France and Germany.* Oxford: Oxford University Press, 1988.

Gregory of Tours, *History of the Franks.* Translated by Lewis Thorpe. New York: Penguin Classics, 1983.

Jerome, Jerome K. *Three Men in a Boat.* New York: Penguin Popular Classics, 1994.

Klingshirn, William E. *Caesarius of Arles.* Cambridge: Cambridge University Press, 1994.

Oppenheimer, Stephen. *Out of Eden.* London: Constable and Robinson Ltd, 2004.

Previte-Orton, C. W. *Shorter Cambridge Medieval History.* Cambridge: Cambridge University Press, 1952.

Shakespeare, William. *The Complete Works.* Edited by Stanley Wells and Gary Taylor. Oxford: Oxford University Press, 1988.

Shirer, William L. *The Rise and Fall of the Third Reich.* New York: Simon and Schuster, 1960.

Strayer, Joseph R., editor-in-chief. *Dictionary of the Middle Ages*, 12 volumes. New York: Charles Scribner's Sons, 1983.

Suetonius. *The Twelve Caesars.* Translated by Robert Graves. New York: Penguin Classics, 1957.

Trevelyn, G. M. *A Shortened History of England.* New York: Penguin Books, 1942.

Wallace-Hadrill, J. M. *The Barbarian West 400–1000*. Malden, MA: Blackwell, 1967, 1985.

——————. *The Long-Haired Kings.* Toronto: University of Toronto Press and Medieval Academy of America, 1982.

Waugh, Evelyn. *Brideshead Revisited.* New York: Penguin Books, 1945.

About the Author

Christine Kaferly has worked for over twenty years in systems engineering, starting her career in electro-optics. Perhaps her scientific background and engineering work, which has a lot to do with observation, integration, and documentation, has led her to write about her travels. But her love of travel, her interest in history, and her enjoyment of learning are the driving forces in her life. Every spring she is filled with wanderlust, and begins to plan a travel project. Her predilection towards European culture and history does not mean she is limiting herself, but aspires to achieve world-class traveller status. She lives in Colorado, and spends as much time as possible planning trips, travelling, reading, and writing about her travels.